A GARDENER'S GUIDE TO

Herbs

Editor Valerie Duncan
Series Editor Graham Strong

INDEX

CONTENTS

KEY TO 'AT A GLANCE' TABLES

SOWING/PLANTING   HARVESTING

'At a glance' tables are your quick guide.
For full information, consult the accompanying text.

LEFT: A formal herb garden need not be very large or elaborate. Here a simple cross pattern of brick paths is centred on a lead statue and framed in cotton lavender.

ABOVE: The pretty leaves of tansy.

3

GROWING HERBS

No garden is complete without a few herbs, which are mainly used to add flavour and delight to food, but which have many other uses too: in cosmetics, craft arrangements, herbal remedies and as good companions and edging plants in the garden. You can buy them, of course, but you will feel extra pride when using herbs you have grown yourself.
And herbs are almost all very easy to grow.

To a botanist a herb is a plant that does not have a permanent woody stem: that is, one that is not a tree or shrub. Its edibility is irrelevant. Gardeners have a different definition. To them, a herb is a plant that can be added to food or used for medicinal purposes, even if the plant in question is actually a shrub, such as rosemary, or even a tree, such as the bay tree. Herbs are (or may be) used fresh, unlike spices, which are almost always dried or prepared in some other way first. (Spices, such as pepper or nutmeg, are the seeds, flowers, bark or roots of tropical trees or shrubs.)

LEFT: A pink and grey border of pinks, lavender and thyme harmonises in this herb garden with old-fashioned roses, although they are not yet in bloom.

THE RICH GREEN COLOUR and the soft texture of parsley makes as elegant a garnish for flowers as it does for a dinner plate. In this stunning garden it is used as contrast with miniature blue violas and white sweet alyssum.

USING HERBS

Today we use herbs most often when preparing food. Any cook knows how useful it is to have some herbs on hand. Even a pinch of dried herbs from a supermarket packet can make a great difference to a mediocre dish, but the same herbs fresh from the garden can add the savour and scent that makes the dish something special. Restraint, however, should be the order of the day. The recipe will be your guide, but remember that dried herbs are often sharper in flavour than fresh ones and fresh herbs vary in strength with the season. Add a little at a time, tasting as you go: you don't want to taste the herb before you taste the food. Go easy, too, in planning the menu. One herbed item on the plate is usually sufficient.

Herbs are used extensively in flower arrangements and crafts, where they add fragrance and different textures. Herbal pot-pourris and wall hangings are especially effective and herbs can be used in home-made cosmetics for those who want an alternative to commercial preparations.

Herbs are also credited with all sorts of medicinal qualities. In the past it was an essential part of a doctor's education to learn to distinguish beneficial herbs from useless and harmful ones, and these studies laid the foundation of the modern science of botany. Some of the old prescriptions have been verified by science and many modern drugs are still extracted from plants, although other old remedies were apparently based on nothing more than wishful thinking and superstition. (Sometimes the patient may have been merely suffering from a shortage of vitamins which a salad of green herbs made good.) The folklore attached to herbs is part of their charm, but don't dabble in herbal cures without seeking advice from your doctor or a reputable herbalist first.

HARVESTING HERBS

The traditional way to gather herbs is to pick them just as they are coming into flower (when the flavour is strongest) and use them immediately. This way you use them at their best and most attractive.

Many herbs can also be used after they have been dried. You can spread them out on a table to dry in the shade for a couple of days or, these days, the microwave oven provides a more than acceptable alternative. Gather the herbs, spread them on a paper towel, cover them with another paper towel, and zap them with the full power of the microwave for a minute or two. Check them, and if they aren't quite dry, give them some more time with the top towel off. The precise timing depends on what sort of herb it is and how dry the leaves were to start with.

Alternatively, you can freeze the fresh herbs. Just put them in a freezer bag, pop them in the freezer and take what you want when you need them.

CHOOSING HERBS TO GROW

Whether you plan to plant an extensive collection of herbs or just a few, your first choices will obviously include the ones you like best, those that feature in your favourite recipes or craft activities. (Chances are you'll probably already have them, dried, in your kitchen.) It is probably a good idea to grow several plants of these herbs to avoid harvesting them to death. However, don't let unfamiliarity stop you from trying out a plant or two of a herb with looks or fragrance that appeal to you.

PLANTING HERBS

It is a time-honoured tradition to grow herbs in gardens of their own, and if you have the enthusiasm and the space, a small formal herb garden with its beds divided by paths arranged around a central feature such as a statue or a sundial can be very pretty. Most herbs are low growing, and few are all that distinguished in appearance – indeed, some are rather nondescript. Marshalling them into formal beds flatters them, and you can play their subtle foliage colours and textures off against one another. You might, for instance, contrast the grey leaves of sage with the lush green ones of parsley, or the featheriness of dill with the solidity of rosemary; and the variegated and fancy-leaved versions of such herbs as sage, balm or mint will enrich your palette.

If a formal garden is not for you, don't despair. There will be a place for herbs in any garden, for they really are very adaptable. Try one of the following ideas.
• Plant herbs in your flower beds. Being mostly low growing, they are best planted at the front, where their subtle greens and greys will set off the bright flowers behind.
• Plant them along the edges of your paths, where they will release their scent on the air as you brush past.
• They can look especially good in front of roses – and they will hide the rose bushes' thorny legs – but be careful if you have to spray the roses. You won't want the spray drifting onto the herbs and rendering them dangerous to eat.
• Be strictly utilitarian and plant them to edge the beds in the vegetable garden. Here they will give you something to look at when the beds are bare between crops.
• Most varieties grow very well in pots, which means that even if all the garden you have is an apartment balcony you can still have the pleasure of fresh herbs.
• Give your herbs a windowbox on the kitchen windowsill so that you can just reach out and harvest as you need them – but only if the window gets the sun, and make sure they are outside in the fresh air. Magazines are full of pictures of pots of herbs growing in the kitchen itself, but herbs are not indoor plants. They survive inside for a few weeks, but they get straggly and leggy and you won't get much of a harvest.
• However you choose to grow herbs in your garden, don't plant them too far from the kitchen door. Nothing is more frustrating than to find you need a sprig or two for some dish and have to make an expedition to the bottom of the garden while a pot boils over.

PROPAGATION

Most herbs can be grown from seed, but it can be a slow process and most gardeners start with purchased seedlings or by taking cuttings or dividing plants. The appropriate method for each plant is discussed under its entry.

MAINTENANCE

Growing herbs is easy. As a general rule, they love sunshine and don't need much watering: indeed the flavour is richest if they aren't encouraged to grow too lush. They don't, however, appreciate being starved so give them good, well-drained soil and some fertiliser occasionally. The main exceptions to the rule are basil and chives, which do best with generous feeding and regular watering, and bergamot and the various mints, which are lovers of damp soil. Most herbs have few specific pest or disease problems. You'll find more detail about requirements and problems in the description of each species.

STRIKING A CUTTING

If you are going to strike a herb from a cutting, take the cutting from a strong, healthy plant early in the morning. The cutting should be 5–10cm (2–4in) long. If you are not able to plant it at once, stand it in water so that it does not wilt.

Remove the lower leaves and prepare a small pot with a mix of two-thirds coarse sand and one-third potting compost. Make a hole with your finger or a pencil where the cutting is to go, insert the cutting to about one-third of its length and firm the mix around it. Water well and then cover the pot with a plastic bag to create a mini-greenhouse.

Keep the mix damp but not wet. Once roots have formed, the plant can be planted out in the garden.

1. TO TAKE A STEM CUTTING, cut just below a leaf (node or joint). Do not bruise the stem, and trim the end of the cutting with a razor blade if need be. Prepare a pot, filling it with compost then tapping it to settle the compost.

2. INSERT ALL THE CUTTINGS into a pot (or several pots), first making a hole in the compost with your finger for each cutting and then firming the compost gently around the cuttings. Space the cuttings around the edge of the pot.

3. THEN WATER THE CUTTINGS in well but gently, taking care not to dislodge them. Make sure the container has adequate drainage holes so that the excess water will drain away. If the soil remains too wet, the cuttings will rot.

4. MAKE A WIRE OR BAMBOO FRAME that fits around the pot and is tall enough to clear the cuttings. Place a polythene bag over the frame and pot: the bag will keep the air and soil moist. Place the pot in a position that is out of direct sunlight.

ALCHEMILLA
Alchemilla vulgaris

FEATURES

Alchemilla vulgaris (A. xanthochlora), the wild lady's mantle, is a hardy perennial native to the mountains of Europe, Asia and America. It grows to 23–45cm (9–18in) and has rounded pale green leaves, with lobed and toothed edges that collect the dew or raindrops. The water thus collected once was reputed to have healing and magical powers. Feathery heads of yellow-green flowers are produced in early summer and can continue into autumn. More popular, and very widely grown as a garden plant, is *Alchemilla mollis* which is very similar in both appearance and properties. The alpine lady's mantle, *Alchemilla alpina*, a smaller plant growing to 15cm (6in), is also said to have similar, but more effective, properties.

CONDITIONS

Aspect   Lady's mantle will grow in sun or moderate shade.

Site   It is tolerant of most soils except waterlogged conditions.

GROWING METHOD

Sowing and planting   Lady's mantle self-seeds freely and removing and replanting self-sown seedlings is an easy way to get new plants. Seed can be sown in early spring or autumn. Germination takes about two or three weeks but can be erratic. Autumn-sown seedlings will need to be overwintered under glass. Plant them out in spring 45cm (18in) apart. Established plants can be propagated by division either in spring or autumn.

Feeding   The lady's mantles are tolerant plants, but be careful to avoid overwatering. Mulch alchemillas lightly in the spring and the autumn and apply a balanced general fertiliser in spring.

THE 'LADY' to whom the name Lady's Mantle refers, was the Virgin Mary, to whom the herb was dedicated during medieval times.

Problems   None.

Pruning   Cut back flowerheads as they start to fade to prevent self-seeding. Cut back dead foliage in late autumn.

HARVESTING

Picking   Young leaves can be picked as required throughout the summer, after the morning dew has dried.

Storage   Leaves can be dried and stored in airtight dark glass jars.

Freezing   Not suitable for freezing.

USES

Culinary   Young leaves can be added to salads in small amounts. They have a mild, but somewhat bitter taste.

Medicinal   In medieval times the lady's mantle was dedicated to the Virgin Mary, and was considered to be particularly a woman's herb, as it was used to treat a wide range of womens' problems, including menstrual problems, menopause, breastfeeding, and inflammations. It was also used as a wound healer for external use, and to make a mouth rinse for use after tooth extraction.

Cosmetic   Lady's mantle can be used to make a soothing and healing rinse that is good for skin complaints.

Gardening   Alchemilla is widely used as an edging plant as well as being grown in flower borders, and the attractive feathery heads of yellow-green flowers are particularly popular with flower arrangers.

ALCHEMILLA AT A GLANCE

A pretty perennial with rounded leaves and feathery flowerheads, it was traditionally a woman's herb. Hardy to minus 15°C.

JAN	/		
FEB	/		*Parts used*
MAR	plant		Leaves
APR	plant		Flowers
MAY	plant	harvest	
JUN		harvest	*Uses*
JULY		harvest	Culinary
AUG		harvest	Medicinal
SEPT	plant	harvest	Cosmetic
OCT	/		Gardening
NOV	/		
DEC	/		

ALOE VERA
Aloe barbadensis, syn. *A. vera*

FEATURES

A bitter-juiced, succulent half hardy perennial, aloe vera can be stood outside in the summer or grown as a houseplant. It grows to about 60cm (2ft) high, or less in containers where growth is restricted. A strong, fibrous rooting system supports a single, sturdy stem. The fleshy, pale green leaves are lanceolate with spiny, toothed edges. The pendent, bell-shaped flowers are yellowish-orange.

CONDITIONS

Aspect   Outdoors, aloe vera needs a frost-free position in full sun or part shade, sheltered from cold winds. Indoors, grow it on a sunny windowsill, and at a minimum temperature of 10°C.

Site   Outdoors, grow aloe vera in a fertile, free-draining soil, and when cultivated indoors as a houseplant, grow it in John Innes No 2 compost with 25 per cent extra grit added.

GROWING METHOD

Sowing and planting   Aloe vera can be propagated by removing the offsets from the base of a mature plant. Pot these up in a mix of 2 parts compost to 1 part sharp sand. It can also be propagated by seed. Germination can be erratic, taking from 4 to 24 months. A temperature of 21°C needs to be maintained during germination.

Feeding   Do not overwater; in the wild it is used to alternate wet and dry periods. Allow the plant to become fairly dry in between waterings and water only very lightly during winter. Water more often during the growing period when the leaves and stem begin to thicken. Do not mulch plants as this could cause stem rot. Indoor plants should be given a feed of a liquid fertiliser monthly. Excessive feeding may slow growth.

Problems   Watch out for root rot in wet soils. Aphids,

LIKE MOST SUCCULENTS, aloe vera grows very well as a pot plant on a sunny windowsill. Its pale flowers are not very exciting.

scale insects and mealy bugs can be a problem.

Pruning   The plant grows from the centre, and so the older, outside leaves need to be cut to keep the plant in balance and in shape. These leaves do not grow back once cut.

HARVESTING

Picking   Harvest leaves as required but always cut larger, lower leaves first as they have more juice. This also promotes new growth from the centre. Trim the thorny edges of the leaves and split the leaf across its width to extract the gooey gel. As the gel ceases to flow, scratch the exposed leaf and continue to do so until only the green leaf skin is left. Older leaves tend to have stronger properties.

Storage   Whole or partially used leaves can be wrapped in foil and stored in the refrigerator for several days, or the extracted juice can be bottled.

Freezing   Can be frozen for 6 months.

USES

Cosmetic   The juice of the leaves is applied directly to the skin as a softening agent. Astringent and drying, it is often combined with lanolin and vitamins A and E to intensify its soothing qualities. It is used in many commercial cosmetic preparations.

Medicinal   The gel is a remarkable healer and can be applied to soothe and heal minor wounds (insect bites, scratches and cuts) and sunburn. *Caution:* always seek medical attention for serious burns. Other, ornamental, species of aloe do not have the same properties as aloe vera, and some contain very astringent sap.

ALOE VERA AT A GLANCE

Perennial succulent grown for the healing gel obtained from the leaves. Usually grown as a houseplant. Not hardy: to 10°C.

JAN		harvest	*Parts used*
FEB		harvest	Leaves
MAR		harvest	
APR		harvest	*Uses*
MAY		harvest	Medicinal
JUN	plant	harvest	Cosmetic
JULY	plant	harvest	
AUG	plant	harvest	
SEPT		harvest	
OCT		harvest	
NOV		harvest	
DEC		harvest	

ANGELICA
Angelica archangelica

FEATURES

Growing up to 2m (6ft 6in) tall with a spread of around 1.5m (5ft), angelica is a majestic, stout-stemmed, biennial or short-lived perennial herb (it may continue for several years if prevented from flowering). It has big, toothed leaves made up of several leaflets. The tiny, honey-scented, greenish-white flowers are produced in clusters in early summer; winged seeds follow in late summer. All parts of angelica are subtly, sweetly aromatic.

CONDITIONS

Aspect   Grows best in light shade, sheltered from wind.
Site   Needs deep, well-drained but moisture retentive and fertile soil. In the wild, angelica often grows in damp woodlands or by streams.

GROWING METHOD

Sowing and planting   Can be grown from seed sown as soon as it is ripe. (Seeds will lose viability within about 3 months.) Sow in open ground where they are to flower. Alternatively, sprinkle seeds onto a tray of moist seed compost and barely cover. Keep evenly moist. Expect germination in 3–4 weeks but germination is not always reliable. For a few plants, lift 2-year-old plants in early spring and divide roots into smaller sections. Replant into loose, friable, fertile soil.

Feeding   Keep soil moist and pay particular attention to watering in summer. The plant is native to cool, rainy areas and does not tolerate dryness. Apply a balanced general fertiliser once in early spring when new growth begins and again in early summer. Mulch around plants with compost or well-rotted manure to feed and condition the soil.

Problems   Blackfly may sometimes be a problem. Treat

ACCORDING TO LEGEND, the healing properties of angelica were revealed to a medieval hermit by the angel Raphael – hence the name.

with liquid horticultural soap.

Pruning   No pruning is necessary. In cooler areas it dies back to the ground each winter.

HARVESTING

Picking   Collect the seeds by harvesting the whole flowerhead just as it ripens. Place in a paper bag in a warm, dry place until the seeds fall from the head. Separate the seeds from the dross before storing. For best flavour, cut stems after bloom, but leaves may be picked at any time. Roots are dug straight after flowering and washed clean immediately.

Storage   Store seeds in an airtight jar. Crystallise stems before storage; dry and grind leaves before storing in airtight containers. Store clean roots in a cool, dry, dark and airy place until needed.

Freezing   No parts of the plant are suitable for freezing.

USES

Culinary   Crystallised stems and leaves are used as sweets and to decorate cakes. Leaves can also be used to make a herbal tea. Seeds are used in baking and to flavour drinks.

Medicinal   Tea made from any part of the plant can be taken to soothe nervous conditions and to ward off colds. *Caution:* avoid frequent or heavy consumption of any part of the angelica plant as it can exacerbate certain medical conditions. Diabetics should avoid the plant altogether.

Gardening   Angelica is a handsome plant that makes an attractive addition to a planting of perennial flowers at the back of a border. *Caution:* wild angelica can be confused with water dropwort which is poisonous.

ANGELICA AT A GLANCE

Tall, handsome perennial, the leaves and stems of which can be crystallised to make 'sweets'. Hardy to minus 15°C or below.

JAN	/		
FEB	/		*Parts used*
MAR	plant 🖐		Leaves
APR	plant 🖐		Stems
MAY	plant 🖐	harvest 🌿	Seeds
JUN		harvest 🌿	Roots
JULY		harvest 🖐	
AUG		harvest 🌿	*Uses*
SEPT	plant 🖐	harvest 🌿	Culinary
OCT	plant 🖐	harvest 🌿	Medicinal
NOV	/		Gardening
DEC	/		

ANISE
Pimpinella anisum

FEATURES

A dainty, feathery-looking annual that will reach a height of 45–60cm (18–24in), anise has rounded, mid-green leaves with distinctly toothed edges. The flat heads of white flowers appear during summer and are then followed by the small, licorice flavoured seeds – aniseeds.

CONDITIONS

Aspect   Anise needs full sun and a site sheltered from strong winds which will flatten this light, airy herb.

Site   Light, sandy, well-drained soil enriched with well-rotted organic matter is ideal for this plant but anise grows well enough in any friable, well-drained soil.

GROWING METHOD

Sowing and planting   When spring has definitely turned warm, sow seeds where they are to grow about 8mm (0.25in) deep and 15cm (6in) apart. For its seeds to ripen properly, anise requires a long, hot summer and in cooler areas where summers may be short or mild it is advisable to start seedlings early. Sow them indoors in late winter or early spring into trays of seed compost. Place in a sunny window in a heated propagator and keep lightly moist. When seedlings are big enough to handle, prick out into small individual pots and place these in the propagator. Plant out only when all danger of frost has passed.

Feeding   Anise needs moisture around its roots at all times and must never be allowed to dry out. To avoid flattening the stems, water the soil rather than the leaves. Grown in average well-drained garden soil and mulched with well-rotted manure or compost, anise will not need further feeding. If soil is friable but poor, rake

THE ROMANS flavoured wedding cakes with anise, thus starting (it is sometimes said) the tradition of rich cakes at wedding banquets.

in a ration of a balanced general fertiliser at planting time and mulch when the seedlings are 20cm (8in) tall.

Problems   No particular problems.

HARVESTING

Picking   When the flowers have finished, the seeds will begin to grow and ripen. When fully ripe, remove the seedheads and place them on paper or in a container in the sun to dry out. Don't allow dew to settle on them overnight or expose them to rain. Fresh leaves can be picked as they are needed.

Storage   When the seedheads are fully dry, rub the seeds to separate them from the husks and store them in airtight jars.

Freezing   Not suitable for freezing.

USES

Culinary   Seeds give a pleasant, licorice taste to many types of cooked foods including cakes and pies, stewed fruits and vegetable dishes. The seeds are also said to be an aid to digestion. Fresh leaves may be used in salads or added late to casseroles, stews and soups.

Medicinal   Aniseed is a good tonic for the digestive system and regular intake of aniseed is said to help prevent colds and to banish bad breath. If taken before bed, aniseed will encourage sound sleep.

Craft   Aniseed is used in pot-pourris and pomanders.

Gardening   Anise is strongly attractive to both bees and butterflies and will attract them to the garden.

ANISE AT A GLANCE

A dainty, feathery-looking annual grown for the small, licorice-flavoured seeds – aniseeds. Frost hardy to minus 5°C.

Month	Activity		Parts used
JAN	/		Seeds
FEB	/		Leaves
MAR	plant		
APR	plant		
MAY	plant	harvest	*Uses*
JUN	plant	harvest	Culinary
JULY		harvest	Medicinal
AUG		harvest	Craft
SEPT		harvest	Gardening
OCT	/		
NOV	/		
DEC	/		

ANISE HYSSOP
Agastache foeniculum

FEATURES

Anise hyssop, or agastache, is a perennial herb, similar to mint in appearance, but with a somewhat neater, clump-forming habit, and growing to about 60–90cm (2–3ft). The mid-green, nettle-shaped leaves have an aniseed scent. Long spikes of purple flowers, attractive to bees and butterflies, are produced from mid summer onwards. A native of North America, it is not quite as hardy as the better known European members of the mint family. Although perennial, it tends to be short-lived and is best propagated every year, or at least every three years.

CONDITIONS

Aspect
Anise hyssop needs full sun (although it may tolerate a little light shade in mild areas) and shelter from cold winds. It may need winter protection if the temperature drops below about -5°C.

Site
It grows best in a rich, moisture-retentive soil, although it will grow in most garden soils if given a sunny position.

GROWING METHOD

Sowing and planting
Anise hyssop can easily be propagated by division in spring and also by seed and cuttings. The seeds need warmth to germinate and are best sown under glass in spring. Germination takes approximately 10–20 days. Prick out the seedlings when they are large enough to handle and plant out in mid spring at about 45cm (18in) apart. Seed can also be sown outdoors in autumn when the soil is warm, but the young plants will need winter protection. Cuttings can be taken in mid to late summer, and the rooted cuttings can be overwintered in a greenhouse or cold frame

BEES AND BUTTERFLIES are attracted to the tall purple-blue flower spikes of anise hyssop, borne from mid summer onwards.

and then planted out in spring.

Feeding
Do not allow to dry out. Keep well watered in summer. Mulch lightly in spring and autumn and apply a balanced general fertiliser in spring.

Problems
Anise hyssop rarely suffers from pests or disease, except that seedlings may damp off and the plants may suffer from mildew in hot summers.

Pruning
Cut back old flowerheads and woody growth in autumn to keep plants compact and to prevent them becoming straggly.

HARVESTING

Picking
Pick the young leaves just before the plant flowers. Cut flowers just as they are beginning to open.

Storage
Dry leaves in a cool, airy space and store in dark, airtight, glass jars.

Freezing
Put leaves in a freezer bag; freeze for up to 6 months.

USES

Culinary
The leaves can be used to make a refreshing aniseed-flavoured tea. They can also be used, like borage, in summer fruit cups, and can be added to salads and used as a seasoning, particularly in savoury pork and rice dishes. The flowers will add colour to salads and fruit cups.

Craft
The scented leaves of anise hyssop can be used in pot-pourri.

Gardening
Anise hyssop is an excellent bee herb. Attractive white-flowered varieties, 'Alabaster' and 'Alba', are also available.

AGASTACHE AT A GLANCE

A perennial herb, very similar to mint in appearance, and with a refreshing aniseed flavour. Hardy to minus 5 to minus 10°C.

Month	Activity		Parts used
JAN	/		Leaves
FEB	/		Flowers
MAR	plant		
APR	plant		
MAY	plant	harvest	*Uses*
JUN		harvest	Culinary
JULY	plant	harvest	Craft
AUG	plant	harvest	Gardening
SEPT	plant		
OCT	/		
NOV	/		
DEC	/		

BAY TREE
Laurus nobilis

FEATURES

An aromatic, evergreen tree reaching about 7–12m (23–40ft) high. It can be pruned hard to reduce size, or clipped for topiary, and is often grown in containers where the height can be controlled. The trunk has smooth, grey bark and the short stalks bear alternate, shiny, dark green, elliptical-shaped leaves with wavy edges. The leaves are 3–6cm (1.25–2.5in) long and leathery in texture and are the edible part of the plant. The inconspicuous yellowish-green flowers, which appear in spring, produce dark purple or black, one-seeded berries.

CONDITIONS

Aspect Grow in a sunny site, sheltered from cold winds. In cold areas, give extra protection or bring container plants indoors.

Site Needs moderately rich and well-drained soil. Grow container plants in John Innes No 2 and ensure that the pot is large enough for the root ball. Add well-rotted farmyard manure or compost to improve beds before planting. Mulching is always beneficial.

GROWING METHOD

Sowing and planting Not often grown successfully from seed; cuttings taken in late summer offer the best chance of success. Take a 7.5cm (3in) cutting from a mature plant and remove the upper and lower leaves. Dip in hormonal rooting powder. Place in a small pot of two-thirds coarse sand and one-third potting compost. Place the pot under a plastic bag, making a wire frame to hold the bag off the cutting. Cuttings may take 9 months to root. Bay can also be propagated by layering the lower branches in late summer.

Feeding Bays tolerate dry conditions: let the soil dry out between waterings. However, during hot weather keep the moisture up, and pay special attention to specimens in containers. Apply a balanced general fertiliser once in spring, and then mulch with well-rotted organic matter. Keep mulch away from the trunk.

Problems Scale, a small wingless insect covered with a waxy substance, may suck the sap of the plant and cause stunted growth. Secretions attract ants, promoting sooty mould. Treat with insecticidal soap sprays.

Pruning Pruning is only necessary if you want to restrict the height or formalise the shape. However, bay responds well to clipping once or twice a year.

HARVESTING

Picking Leaves may be picked early in the day throughout the year, and then used fresh or dried as required.

LEAVES OF THE BAY TREE crowned the brows of ancient heroes, and it is an old belief that no harm can come to a house where it grows.

Storage Dry in dark, airy room. Place leaves on a firm, flat surface and weigh them to prevent curling. Store dried leaves in sealed jars.

Freezing Freeze dried leaves up to 6 months.

USES

Culinary Excellent as a flavouring in soups, stews, sauces and custards. Bay is also used when cooking game, in terrines and in pickling brines. Bay leaves are an essential component of the bouquet garni.

Medicinal An infusion of leaves will aid digestion.

Gardening This slow-growing tree casts dense shade. It is sometimes pruned into formal shapes, and is outstanding as a container specimen.

BAY AT A GLANCE

An evergreen tree with glossy green aromatic leaves much used in cooking. Frost hardy to minus 10-15°C if out of cold winds.

			Parts used
JAN		harvest	Leaves
FEB		harvest	
MAR		harvest	
APR	plant	harvest	
MAY	plant	harvest	*Uses*
JUN		harvest	Culinary
JULY		harvest	Medicinal
AUG		harvest	Gardening
SEPT		harvest	
OCT		harvest	
NOV		harvest	
DEC		harvest	

BASIL

Ocimum basilicum, O. sanctum

SOME COOKS think purple-leaved basil 'Dark Opal' is less sweetly flavoured than the ordinary green one; others detect no difference.

THE FLOWERS of the common green basil are not very exciting, and some people prefer to pinch them off to promote more luxuriant foliage.

PLANT BASIL where you sit in summer and you won't be bothered with flies or mosquitoes. This is the 'cinnamon-scented' variety.

FEATURES

Basils are sub-tropical species, mostly grown as half-hardy annuals in temperate climates. Many varieties are available including sweet or common basil (*O. basilicum*), lemon basil (*O. basilicum* 'Citriodorum'), bush basil (*O. basilicum* 'Minimum') and sacred or holy basil (*O. sanctum*). All basils have an overriding and specific aroma and taste, depending on the variety. Their colours range from yellow-green to dark green and purple, and the small, white flowers that appear in summer produce tiny, dark brown seeds. Sweet basil grow into a bushy plant, 30–60cm (1–2ft) tall, and has silky-leaved stems. The ruffle-leaf and lettuce-leaf varieties have crinkly leaves. Coloured leaved forms such as *O. basilicum* 'Purpurescens' make decorative plants. Bush basil (*O. basilicum* 'Minimum') is a compact, small-leaved plant, growing 15cm (6in) tall. Most basils make ideal pot plants.

CONDITIONS

Aspect   Basil needs a sunny, sheltered, frost-free position. In colder areas, it is best grown under cover in a greenhouse or cold frame or on a sunny kitchen windowsill.

Site   Needs rich, moist, well-drained soils that are not too acid. Add plenty of well-rotted compost or farmyard manures when preparing beds. Lime in autumn if required. Mulch soil during very hot or dry weather, but not until the soil has warmed up as basil roots need heat for growth.

GROWING METHOD

Sowing and planting   Sow seed in late spring to early summer in a warm, sunny, sheltered position after all danger of frost has passed. Germination is usually quick. Thin out seedlings to 15cm (6in) apart. In most areas seeds are better sown under glass in early spring. Sow the seed in seed trays using a good quality seed compost, preferably putting them in a propagator with some bottom heat. Cover the tray with clear plastic to hasten the process. Transfer the seedlings three to a 9cm (3.5in) pot after two weeks, and then transplant them into open beds or containers from early summer onwards.

Feeding   Water regularly as basil likes moisture. Feed occasionally with a nitrogen-rich liquid fertiliser, especially if the plants are growing in containers.

Problems   Some beetles and slugs feed on leaves and stems causing extensive damage to the foliage. Remove the pests by hand or set shallow beer traps in damp soil among the plants.

Pruning   Pinch out the growing tips to inhibit flowering and promote a bushier plant.

IF YOU LOVE FRESH BASIL in cooking, you will want to grow plenty of it. Planting some in containers means that the plants can be brought under cover in bad weather, or can be grown on the kitchen windowsill, to give a much longer cropping period.

HARVESTING

Picking   Fresh leaves can be picked at any time or harvested and dried during late summer. Whole sprigs may also be cut after the flower buds have formed but before they open.

Storage   Leaves and sprigs may be preserved in oils or vinegars. Leaves can also be dried and stored in airtight jars. Bunches can be placed in water and kept for a few days in the refrigerator.

Freezing   Put the sprigs in a freezer bag. They can be frozen for up to 6 months.

USES

Culinary   Basil is a very popular culinary herb, especially in Italian, Mediterranean and Thai cuisines. Leaves and flowers are used in salads or as an aromatic garnish. The leaves are also used in combination with other herbs in tomato, vegetable and meat dishes and to make pesto. Leaves and sprigs may be preserved in oils, vinegars or butters, where they add their own particular lemon, cinnamon or varietal flavour.

Medicinal   Basil tea is a useful remedy for travel sickness. A crushed leaf rubbed on the skin is said to repel mosquitos.

Craft   Basil can be used in pot-pourris and sachets.

The flowering stems are sometimes used in small bouquets and other floral arrangements such as wreaths.

Gardening   Basil is a popular companion plant with organic gardeners, who believe that planting it next to tomatoes and capsicum will improve their growth. Keep a pot of basil in the kitchen to act as an insect repellent.

BASIL AT A GLANCE

Annual herbs in many different varieties, with leaves in a range of colours, scents and flavours. Tender. Protect from frost.

		Parts used
JAN	/	Leaves
FEB	/	Sprigs
MAR	/	
APR	/	
MAY	plant harvest	*Uses*
JUN	plant harvest	Culinary
JULY	plant harvest	Medicinal
AUG	harvest	Craft
SEPT	/	Gardening
OCT	/	
NOV	/	
DEC	/	

BERGAMOT
Monarda didyma

FEATURES

A member of the mint family with a pungent citrus-like flavour, bergamot can reach 60–90cm (2–3ft) in height. The wild bergamot, *Monarda didyma*, also known as bee balm, is a hardy herbaceous perennial, but there are annual, biennial and perennial varieties with brilliant scarlet red, purple, pink or white flowers in summer. Bergamot is semi-dormant during winter, sending up squarish stems in spring bearing dark green, ovate leaves with toothed margins. The flowers attract bees.

CONDITIONS

Aspect Prefers a sunny location; tolerates partial shade.

Site An excellent border plant for moist soil. Grow in a humus-rich soil containing a lot of organic matter. Mulch well with leaves, straw or compost to retain moisture and keep down weeds around this shallow-rooting herb.

GROWING METHOD

Sowing and planting Can be grown from seed, but seeds are very fine and often unreliable – this herb is easily cross-pollinated and plants may not be true to the parent in colour or form. Sow seeds in spring in trays of seed compost, covering the tray with glass. Seeds germinate within 2 weeks. Transplant seedlings to the garden when they are 7.5cm (3in) high. More reliable is root division in spring: take sections of runners or sucker shoots from the outside of the clump, which will have roots throughout the bed. Discard the centre of the clump and pot the other sections. Plant out in the garden when they are growing strongly, 80cm (32in) apart.

Feeding Water well – like all members of the mint family, bergamot requires water at all times. Add general fertiliser to the backfill when planting. Give another application of fertiliser each spring.

Problems Powdery mildew and rust can affect bergamot. Cut back and remove diseased parts.

Pruning In late autumn prune the plant back close to ground level. It will regenerate in spring. To increase the strength of the plant, cut flowerheads before they bloom in the first year. After flowering, the plant may be cut back to within 3cm (1.25in) of the soil surface as this can promote a second flowering in autumn.

HARVESTING

Picking Leaves for making tea are stripped from stems both just before and just after flowering. The colourful flower petals can also be harvested.

Storage Leaves can be part dried in a shady place for 2 or 3 days and then drying can be completed in a very low oven. Flowers do not store well

MOST COLOURFUL OF HERBS, bergamot is indigenous to the Americas. Native Americans brewed Oswego tea from its leaves.

and so should only be picked as required.

Freezing Put sprigs in a freezer bag. They can be frozen for up to 6 months.

USES

Culinary Fresh leaves can be used in summer fruit drinks or punches, and fresh flower petals are good for decorating salads. Leaves are also used for making tea.

Medicinal The herb tea can be used to relieve nausea, flatulence, vomiting, colds, etc.

Craft Dried leaves can be used in pot-pourris. The oil is used in perfumery, to scent candles etc.

Garden The colourful flowers attract bees and this herb is therefore a good companion for plants that need insect pollination.

BERGAMOT AT A GLANCE

Attractive perennial border plant, with aromatic leaves that can be used to make a refreshing tea. Hardy to minus 15°C or below.

JAN	/		
FEB	/		
MAR	plant		
APR	plant		
MAY	plant	harvest	
JUN	plant	harvest	
JULY		harvest	
AUG		harvest	
SEPT	plant	harvest	
OCT	plant		
NOV	/		
DEC	/		

Parts used
Leaves
Flowers

Uses
Culinary
Medicinal
Craft
Gardening

BETONY

Stachys officinalis

A BREW OF BETONY LEAVES was greatly prized by the Romans as a cure for hangovers, but perhaps our wine is different from theirs, for it doesn't seem to be as effective today. It still seems to provide some relief for headaches, though.

FEATURES

Betony is a spreading perennial with many erect stems growing 45–60cm (18–24in) in height. It has hairy, rough-textured, grey-green leaves that are biggest around the base of the plant. Spikes of purplish, pink or white flowers appear on long, lavender-like stems during late spring and summer.

CONDITIONS

Aspect   Originally from Europe and western Asia, betony prefers full sun and an airy, open position.
Site   Any average well-drained garden soil.

GROWING METHOD

Sowing and planting   New plants are most easily established by lifting and dividing a big, mature plant in mid-autumn or, in cold areas, early spring. Replant the divisions, each with its own roots, immediately. Cuttings are another way to start new plants. Take 7.5cm (3in) long cuttings of new growth in late spring. Root them in containers of moist, sandy potting compost and plant them out when about 20cm (8in) tall.
Feeding   Betony will always look and grow best in gardens where the soil is kept evenly moist. If grown in fertile soil, a balanced general fertiliser applied once when new growth begins is all that is needed.
Problems   No particular problems.
Pruning   Pinch out tips of new growth in spring to create a more compact, bushy plant. Cut stems to the ground in late autumn.

HARVESTING

Picking   Pick stems, leaves and flowers in summer.
Storage   Tie cut stems together and hang them upside down in a dark, airy place to dry. Break and crumble the dried parts into airtight jars.
Freezing   Not suitable for freezing.

USES

Medicinal   Tea made from the dried stems, leaves and flowers can relieve headaches and other minor pains. It is said to be a general tonic. *Caution:* do not take roots or fresh leaves internally.
Gardening   Today, betony is grown mostly for its looks. It is an attractive addition to mixed flower borders or can be used informally or to edge paths or formal plantings.

BETONY AT A GLANCE

A spreading perennial with rough, hairy grey-green leaves and spikes of pink or purple flowers. Hardy to minus 15°C or below.

JAN	/	*Parts used*
FEB	/	Leaves
MAR	plant 🖑	
APR	plant 🖑	*Uses*
MAY	plant 🖑	Medicinal
JUN	plant 🖑 harvest 🌾	Gardening
JULY	harvest 🌾	
AUG	harvest 🌾	
SEPT	/	
OCT	plant 🖑	
NOV	/	
DEC	/	

BORAGE
Borago officinalis

FEATURES

A fast-growing annual or biennial growing 60–90cm (2–3ft) tall, borage bears star-shaped flowers with protruding black anthers in summer. They are usually bright sky-blue, although they can sometimes be pink or white. The bush bears many sprawling, leafy branches with hollow stems, which can be quite fragile. The stems are covered with stiff white hairs and the greyish-green leaves are also hairy.

CONDITIONS

Aspect Prefers sunny locations but grows in most positions, including partial shade. It needs plenty of space. The brittle stems may need staking to prevent wind damage.

Site Grows well in most soils that are aerated, moist and mulched to keep weeds down.

GROWING METHOD

Sowing and planting Sow seed directly into the garden and thin out the seedlings later, leaving 60cm (24in) between plants. Seedlings do not transplant well once established. Successive sowings every 3 to 4 weeks will extend the harvesting period. It self-sows readily and its spread may need to be controlled.

Feeding During spells of hot, dry weather borage plants should be kept well watered. Apply a balanced general fertiliser once each spring or use controlled-release granules.

Problems Blackfly can be a problem. Treat with liquid horticultural soap. Mildew may also be a problem late in the year. If so, plants are best dug up and removed.

HARVESTING

Picking Pick the leaves as required while they are fresh and young. *Caution:* handling fresh leaves may cause contact dermatitis. Use gloves. Harvest the open flowers during the summer months.

Storage The leaves must be used fresh; they cannot be dried and stored. The flowers can be crystallised and then stored in airtight jars.

Freezing The leaves cannot be frozen. The flowers may be frozen in ice cubes.

USES

Culinary Borage has a faintly cucumberish taste and leaves can be added to salads, and drinks such as Pimms. Flowers may be frozen in ice cubes for cold drinks, used raw on salads, or to decorate cakes and desserts if crystallised. *Caution:* it may be a danger to health. It is now under study because of the presence of alkaloids.

IN THIS GARDEN blue borage and white garlic grow side by side. In the old days, soldiers ate the flowers of borage to give them courage.

Medicinal Borage tea was used for colds and flu. The leaves and flowers are rich in potassium and calcium. Borage has been found to contain gamma linoleic acid (GLA) and is now being more widely grown as a commercial crop.

Cosmetic The leaves can be used to make a cleansing facial steam.

Craft The flowers can be added to pot-pourri.

Gardening Borage is regarded as an excellent companion plant in the garden, especially when it is planted near strawberries.

BORAGE AT A GLANCE

A tall, fast-growing annual with bristly leaves and small bright blue star-shaped flowers. Hardy to minus 15°C or below.

JAN	/		*Parts used*	
FEB	/			Flowers
MAR	plant 🌱			Leaves
APR	plant 🌱			
MAY	plant 🌱	harvest	*Uses*	
JUN	plant 🌱	harvest		Culinary
JULY		harvest		Medicinal
AUG		harvest		Cosmetic
SEPT		harvest		Craft
OCT	/			Gardening
NOV	/			
DEC	/			

CARAWAY
Carum carvi

CLOSELY RELATED TO CUMIN, caraway has a milder, sweeter flavour but it can be used as a substitute for cumin in many recipes.

FEATURES

Light and airy, caraway is a biennial plant growing to around 60–90cm (2–3ft) in height on slim, faintly striped stems. Leaves are aromatic, finely cut and ferny, and in its second summer the plant produces flat heads of small, white flowers. These are followed by ridged, dark brown, aromatic seeds. The edible, carrot-like roots are white.

CONDITIONS

Aspect   Full sun is best, but caraway will tolerate some shade. In windy areas, shelter is desirable.

Site   Deeply dug, good quality, well-drained soil gives the best results and allows the roots to grow straight and long. Soil that contains well-rotted organic matter is the most fertile.

GROWING METHOD

Sowing and planting   Grow from seed sown in autumn or early spring, directly where the plants are to grow, as the tap root is easily damaged if transplanted. Sow the seeds shallowly, 15–20cm (6–8in) apart, or thin to that spacing after germination. Mulch around the plants with compost or well-rotted manure to condition the soil and conserve the moisture in the soil. Once established it will self-seed.

Feeding   Caraway has no special water needs but will not do well if it is allowed to dry out for long periods. Water deeply during dry times. Rake a ration of a balanced general fertiliser into the soil before planting and water plants with liquid organic or soluble fertiliser once or twice during late spring and summer.

Problems   No particular pest or disease problems but to prevent an invasion of caraway seedlings, remove the seedheads before the seeds fall.

HARVESTING

Picking   Seedheads are picked when thoroughly ripe but before the seeds have begun to fall. To thoroughly dry them, place them in open containers in the sun. Fresh leaves are edible too, but the young, spring leaves are the most palatable. Pick as needed. Roots are also best used when young and small and to harvest, the whole plant should be pulled up in late spring.

Storage   Store dry seeds in airtight jars after separating them from the dried seed head. Roots may be stored in the refrigerator for a few weeks.

Freezing   Caraway is not suitable for freezing.

USES

Culinary   Seeds are used in baking and added to many other recipes, especially vegetable and fruit dishes and curries. They can also be used to make a herbal tea. Leaves may be added to salads, and roots can be steamed or boiled and eaten as a vegetable.

Medicinal   All parts of caraway are good for the digestion and kidneys, and the seeds can be chewed after heavy meals to relieve wind and bloating.

Gardening   Sowing a succession of caraway plants in heavy, not very friable soil improves its tilth.

CARAWAY AT A GLANCE

A delicate, feathery herb, with aromatic foliage and seeds which are used in cooking. Frost hardy to minus 10 to minus 15°C.

Month	Activity		Parts used
JAN	/		Seeds
FEB	/		Leaves
MAR	plant 🌿		Roots
APR	plant 🌿		
MAY	plant 🌿	harvest 🌾	*Uses*
JUN		harvest 🌾	Culinary
JULY		harvest 🌾	Medicinal
AUG		harvest 🌾	Gardening
SEPT	plant 🌿	harvest 🌾	
OCT	/		
NOV	/		
DEC	/		

CATMINT
Nepeta cataria

FEATURES

Nepeta cataria, catmint or catnip, is a perennial, native to Europe and Asia. There are several varieties of catmint grown in gardens, all with slightly different growing habits, including *N. mussinii* and *N. x faassenii*, which have similar properties. In general they are low-growing perennials reaching 30–90cm (1–3ft) in height. Fine white hairs cover both the stem, which is square as in all members of the mint family, and the grey-green leaves. These are coarse-toothed and ovate, although the base leaves are heart-shaped. The tubular summer flowers are massed in spikes or whorls. White, pale pink or purplish blue in colour, they produce very fine seeds. Cats find some catmints very attractive.

CONDITIONS

Aspect   Prefers an open, sunny position but tolerates partial shade. Most fragrant in good sunlight.

Site   Catmint does best in fertile sandy loams.

GROWING METHOD

Sowing and planting   Catmint self-sows readily by seeding, once it is established, and can also be grown from cuttings taken in spring. To do this, cut a 10cm (4in) piece from the parent plant, remove the tip and lower leaves, and place the cutting in a moist soil medium. Cuttings take root in 2 to 3 weeks. Divide mature plants into three or four clumps in spring or autumn.

Feeding   As members of the mint family have a high water requirement, keep this plant moist at all times. Do not stand pots in water, however, as this can drown the plant. Mulch lightly in spring and autumn, and give a balanced general fertiliser in spring. Feed with nitrogen-rich fertiliser such as poultry manure in spring for more leaf growth.

Problems   Catmint is basically pest free.

Pruning   Prune back each year to keep bushes in shape.

HARVESTING

Picking   Pick fresh leaves as required. Cut leafy stems in late summer when the plant is in bloom. Hang them to dry in a cool, shady place.

Storage   Strip leaves and flowers from dried stems and store in airtight jars.

Freezing   Leaves can be put in a freezer bag and frozen for up to 6 months.

USES

Culinary   Fresh young leaves were once a popular salad ingredient and were used for herbal teas, although they are less popular now.

THE POWDER BLUE FLOWERS and softly aromatic leaves of Nepeta x faassenii are most attractive to human eyes and noses.

Medicinal   Catmint was once used as a cold remedy. (The leaves have a high vitamin C content.)

Craft   Dried flowers and leaves are used in pot-pourri mixtures, and in toys for cats.

Gardening   Plant it near vegetables to deter flea beetles. The scent is also said to deter rats.

CATMINT AT A GLANCE

A spreading perennial with aromatic grey-green leaves, it is particularly attractive to cats. Hardy to minus 15°C or below.

JAN	/		
FEB	/		
MAR	plant		
APR	plant		
MAY	plant	harvest	
JUN	plant	harvest	
JULY		harvest	
AUG		harvest	
SEPT	plant	harvest	
OCT	plant		
NOV	/		
DEC	/		

Parts used
- Leaves
- Flowers

Uses
- Culinary
- Medicinal
- Craft
- Gardening

CHAMOMILE

Chamaemelum nobile, syn. *Anthemis nobilis*

CHAMOMILE FLOWERS are pretty but the foliage is attractive in itself. When used as a lawn, plants will tolerate a little wear.

CHAMOMILE GROWS HERE between stepping stones to make an informal path. It gives off fragrance as you walk on it.

FEATURES

This creeping, evergreen perennial herb is known as Roman chamomile and should not to be confused with the erect, taller growing annual form known as German chamomile (*Matricaria recutita*). Both forms have feathery foliage and flower from late spring to late summer. The daisy-like blossoms are white with a yellow centre. Chamomile has an attractive apple-like fragrance and flavour. It forms a dense mat of foliage that can be used to make a 'lawn'.

CONDITIONS

Aspect   Prefers full sun, but grows in partial shade.
Site   Prefers a well-drained, lime-rich soil.

GROWING METHOD

Sowing and planting   Sow the fine seeds in spring in well-fertilised garden beds. Alternatively, sow in trays of seed compost and prick out into 9cm (3.5in) pots. For a chamomile lawn, prepare the area over winter. Sow seed directly into the prepared bed. Rake to cover the seed and water it in. Keep the lawn weeded. Alternatively, cuttings or offshoots taken in spring or autumn can be set out in well-drained soil, 10cm (4in) apart for a lawn or 45cm (18in) apart for flowering plants.

Feeding   Keep soil evenly moist; do not let it dry out. Give light applications of a general fertiliser in spring.

Problems   No specific pests or diseases worry this herb.

Pruning   Chamomile lawns can be cut and clipped and will regenerate quickly.

HARVESTING

Picking   Pick flowers as they appear during late spring and summer, just as the petals start to turn backwards from the central yellow disk.

Storage   Dry flowers on paper on racks in a cool, airy space, and then store them in airtight jars.

Freezing   Flowers can be frozen for up to 6 months.

USES

Culinary   Very popular as a herbal tea.

Medicinal   The tea is good for digestive problems and insomnia. An infusion can be used as mouth wash. A few drops of essential oil in the bath aids relaxation.

Cosmetic   Chamomile flowers are used to make face masks and hair rinses.

Craft   Flowers are used in pot-pourris and pillows.

Gardening   As a companion plant, chamomile keeps a range of other plants healthy, especially cucumber, onions and other herbs. For a good, thick lawn do not allow chamomile to flower. Non-flowering clones, such as 'Treneague' are ideal for lawns.

CHAMOMILE AT A GLANCE

Creeping evergreen herb with aromatic foliage and daisy flowers used to make a popular herb tea. Hardy to minus 15°C or below.

JAN	/		*Parts used*	
FEB	/		Flowers	
MAR	plant			
APR	plant		*Uses*	
MAY	plant	harvest	Culinary	
JUN		harvest	Medicinal	
JULY		harvest	Cosmetic	
AUG		harvest	Craft	
SEPT	plant		Gardening	
OCT	plant			
NOV	/			
DEC	/			

CHERVIL
Anthriscus cerefolium

FEATURES

Chervil is a hardy annual herb that has a long cropping period. Looking rather like parsley, it grows to 30–60cm (1–2ft), the small, light green leaves turning pinkish in hot, sunny weather. Only the lower leaves have stalks. The leaves are usually curly but there is a variety with plain ones. Very small, white flowers are borne in clusters during the summer. The herb has a very subtle flavour, somewhere between anise and parsley.

CONDITIONS

Aspect   Prefers dappled shade during summer. It will quickly run to seed in hot, dry conditions. Ideal for growing indoors.

Site   Chervil needs a moist, rich, light soil.

GROWING METHOD

Sowing and planting   Chervil does not transplant well, and so seeds should be sown into their final position. Cover lightly, even exposing the seeds to the sun a little, but keep moist. Thin seedlings to 25cm (10in) apart when they are 6cm (2.5in) high. Successive plantings every 2 weeks until the weather becomes too hot ensures a long cropping period. In the garden, plant near larger plants to provide shade and protection.

Feeding   Water well as moisture is essential at all times. Occasionally feed with a soluble and nitrogen-rich fertiliser to promote leaf growth.

Problems   Aphids can be a pest. Treat with appropriate sprays as hosing does not seem to work.

HARVESTING

Picking   Chervil leaves are ready to cut from about 6–8 weeks after planting.

CHERVIL AT A GLANCE

An annual herb grown for its pretty, divided leaves which have a flavour between anise and parsley. Hardy to minus 10°C.

JAN	/	*Parts used*
FEB	/	Leaves
MAR	plant 🖑	Stems
APR	plant 🖑	Sprigs
MAY	plant 🖑 harvest 🍃	
JUN	plant 🖑 harvest 🍃	*Uses*
JULY	plant 🖑 harvest 🍃	Culinary
AUG	harvest 🍃	Medicinal
SEPT	harvest 🍃	Cosmetic
OCT	/	
NOV	/	
DEC	/	

THE PRETTY LEAVES of chervil lose their parsley-like flavour when cooked. Sprinkle them over dishes just before serving.

Storage   The leaves are not really suitable for drying: they can be dried rapidly in an oven but they do tend to lose their flavour when undergoing this heating.

Freezing   Herb butters can be wrapped in plastic film and stored in the freezer.

USES

Culinary   Both stems and leaves can be used as a flavouring in foods. Fresh whole sprigs are used in salads or they can also be used to make an attractive garnish. If you are using chervil in cooking, be sure to add it at the end of the cooking process, because long periods of heating will result in it gaining a bitter flavour. Chervil is one of the main ingredients of *fines herbes* used in French cooking. The leaves can be used to make a herb butter.

Medicinal   An infusion of leaves aids digestion and circulatory problems. Fresh leaves can be used to make a poultice for aching joints.

Cosmetic   An infusion of leaves can be used to cleanse skin and improve its suppleness.

CHICORY
Cichorium intybus

FEATURES

This is a large perennial plant, often grown as an annual. It reaches 1–1.5m (3–5ft) or more in height. The intense sky-blue, fine-petalled flowers, borne in summer, open in the morning but close up in the hot midday sun. The broad, oblong leaves with ragged edges, reminiscent of dandelions, form a rosette around the bottom of the tall, straggly stems. The upper leaves are much smaller, giving a bare look to the top of the plant. Some varieties can be cultivated by forcing and blanching, when the lettuce-like heart of the chicory plant turns into chicons.

CONDITIONS

Aspect   Prefers full sun. May need support.
Site   These plants require deep, rich, friable soil for best growth.

GROWING METHOD

Sowing and planting   Sow seeds in spring, into drills or trenches 3cm (1.25in) deep, and thin the seedlings to 30cm (12in) apart when they are established. Seeds may also be germinated in seed trays and seedlings transplanted into the garden during the months of spring.

Feeding   Keep chicory well watered during spells of hot weather. Add compost to the garden bed in mid summer, but do not provide too much nitrogen or the leaves will grow rapidly at the expense of root growth.

Problems   No particular pests or diseases affect this plant.

HARVESTING

Picking   Pick young green leaves of chicory when they are required. Pick newly opened flowers in summer. Dig up roots in autumn.

Storage   The leaves cannot be stored either fresh or dried. The root can be dried and then rendered into a powder.

Freezing   Not suitable for freezing.

Forcing   Lift roots in autumn or winter, trim off the leaves to about 2.5cm (1in) from the root, and keep in the dark in a bucket of dry sand to force sweet, new growth which can be harvested in a few weeks.

USES

Culinary   Use young leaves as soon as they are picked, either in salads or in cooking, and forced leaves as winter salad. The strong, bitterish flavour is similar to dandelion. Flowers can be crystallised and used to decorate cakes and puddings. Roasted chicory root is widely used as a coffee substitute.

CHICORY is thought to have been one of the 'bitter herbs' the Israelites ate with the Passover lamb. Christians thought it was an aphrodisiac.

Medicinal   A bitter tonic and digestive can be made from the leaves, and a laxative from the roots.
Caution: Excessive continued use may cause eye problems.

CHICORY AT A GLANCE

A tall, straggly perennial with intense bright blue flowers, often grown as annual for forcing. Hardy to minus 15°C.

Month	Activity		*Parts used*
JAN	/		Leaves
FEB	/		Flowers
MAR	plant		Roots
APR	plant		Shoots
MAY	plant	harvest	
JUN	plant	harvest	
JULY	plant	harvest	*Uses*
AUG		harvest	Culinary
SEPT		harvest	Medicinal
OCT	force		
NOV	force		
DEC	force		

CHIVES
Allium schoenoprasum, A. tuberosum

GARLIC CHIVES *are taller than regular*
chives and have pretty white flowers.

DAINTY CLUSTERS *of mauve flowers and*
tubular leaves characterise common chives.

CHINESE CHIVES *are eaten as a vegetable*
in China; here we substitute spring onions.

FEATURES

Chives are perennial herbs that make an attractive edging for a herb garden or bed of mixed annuals and perennials. They grow in clumps from very small bulbs that send up 30cm (12in) tall grass-like, hollow, tubular, green leaves, tapering to a point at the top. The plants produce flower stems in summer. The flowers of the common chive, *A. schoenoprasum,* take the form of a dense, globular head of pinkish to pale purple blossoms. Chinese or garlic chives (*A. tuberosum*) have a flowerhead composed of star-like, white flowers and flat, narrow, light to dark green leaves. Chives can be grown successfully in small containers and clumps can even be potted up and brought indoors to keep in the kitchen.

CHIVES AT A GLANCE

This hardy perennial herb is highly valued for its tasty green leaves. Ideal for salads. Hardy to minus 15°C or below.

JAN	/		
FEB	/		
MAR	plant 🖐		*Parts used*
APR	plant 🖐	harvest 🌿	Leaves
MAY	plant 🖐	harvest 🌿	Flowers
JUN	plant 🖐	harvest 🌿	Buds
JULY	plant 🖐	harvest 🌿	
AUG		harvest 🌿	*Uses*
SEPT		harvest 🌿	Culinary
OCT		harvest 🌿	Medicinal
NOV	/		Gardening
DEC	/		

CONDITIONS

Aspect Chives tolerate a wide range of conditions but grow best in a sunny position.
Site Chives do best in rich, moist, but well-drained soil, but will tolerate a wide range of conditions.

GROWING METHOD

Sowing and planting The simplest way to propagate chives is by division. Lift a clump in spring, separate into smaller clumps and replant into fertile ground. Chives can also be grown easily from seed, but need warm conditions to germinate, so are best sown indoors in early spring, with bottom heat. Alternatively, wait until late spring or summer to sow outdoors. Plant clumps 20cm (8in) apart, in rows 30–60cm (1–2ft) apart.

Feeding Water chives well, especially during hot months. At planting time dig in compost or well-rotted manure and a balanced general fertiliser.

Problems Chives can suffer from rust. Cut back and burn diseased growth, or, if bad, remove the plant completely. Mildew may also be a problem, and greenfly may attack pot-grown plants.

HARVESTING

Picking Pick leaves as available. Do not snip off just the tips or the chive will become tough and fibrous. Clip the leaves or blades close to the

BORNE IN LATE SPRING, the flowers make chives one of the most decorative of herbs and a first-rate plant for edging a bed, either in a herb garden or in an old-fashioned cottage garden. Choose plants in flower if possible; some strains are much more richly coloured than others.

ground, leaving about 5cm (2in) still intact. Harvest chives regularly to keep the crop growing. Pick flowers when fully open, but before the colour fades.

Storage Chives do not store very well.

Freezing Leaves can be frozen for about 6 months. Chop them, put them in a freezer bag, and freeze them for use when needed at a later date.

USES

Culinary Leaves of the chive, *A. schoenoprasum,* have a delicate, mild onion flavour and are added to soups or casseroles during the last moments of cooking. Chopped leaves are also used in salads, in herb butter, as a garnish over other vegetables and in the French *fines herbes*. The flowers can be eaten fresh, tossed in salads or made into spectacular herb vinegars or butters. All parts of the Chinese chive, *A. tuberosum,* have a mild garlic flavour and the unopened flower bud has a special place in Asian cuisines.

Medicinal The leaves are mildly antiseptic and also promote digestion.

Gardening Chives are recommended companions for roses, carrots, grapes, tomatoes and fruit trees. They are said to prevent scab on apples and blackspot on roses.

COMFREY
Symphytum officinale

COMFREY LEAVES are handsome but you cannot eat them fresh – they are as rough as sandpaper.

ATTRACTIVE IN GROWTH and in foliage, comfrey makes an unusual tall groundcover. Other species have blue or white flowers.

FEATURES

This large, coarse, hairy perennial grows to 1m (39in) or more high. It has dark green, lanceolate leaves, which reach 25–30cm (10–12in) long, and clusters of bell-shaped flowers in pink-purple or white in summer. The sticky qualities of its rhizome, which is black outside and has juicy white flesh within, gave rise to its nickname of slippery root; its other name, knit-bone, comes from its use in healing. The plant dies down over winter but makes a strong recovery in spring and can be quite invasive in the garden. Confine it to distant parts of the garden where it forms a backdrop.

CONDITIONS

Aspect   Prefers sun or semi-shade, but tolerates most conditions.

Site   Prefers moist, rich soils. Prepare beds with plenty of compost and farmyard manures.

GROWING METHOD

Sowing and planting   Comfrey can be propagated from spring plantings of seed, by root cuttings at any stage of its life cycle or by root division in autumn.

Feeding   Comfrey requires a great deal of water. For best growth mulch in spring and autumn and apply a balanced general fertiliser in spring.

Problems   May suffer from rust or powdery mildew from late summer. Destroy affected parts.

Pruning   Cutting flowers encourages more leaf growth.

HARVESTING

Picking   Leaves can be picked from early summer to autumn. Up to 4 cuttings a year can be taken. Dig up roots in autumn.

Storage   The leaves can be dried and then stored in airtight containers.

Freezing   Can be frozen for 6 months.

USES

Culinary   Not recommended as controversy surrounds the use of young leaves in salads. Dried leaves are sometimes used to make a herbal tea.

Medicinal   The plant contains high concentrations of vitamin B_{12} but a great deal would need to be eaten daily to have any beneficial effect, and some studies suggest that certain alkaloids in the plant can cause chronic liver problems. Roots and leaves are used as a poultice for inflammations, bruises, etc.

Cosmetic   An infusion of leaves makes a cosmetic wash.

Gardening   Comfrey is best used as a liquid manure: steep fresh leaves in water for several weeks. Leaves can also be used to promote decomposition in the compost heap, and so plant it close by.

COMFREY AT A GLANCE

A coarse, hairy, spreading perennial, which can be used to make an excellent organic fertiliser. Hardy to minus 15°C or below.

Month	Activity		Parts used
JAN	/		
FEB	/		Leaves
MAR	plant		Roots
APR	plant		
MAY	plant	harvest	*Uses*
JUN	plant	harvest	
JULY	plant	harvest	(Culinary)
AUG	plant	harvest	Medicinal
SEPT	plant	harvest	Cosmetic
OCT	plant	harvest	Gardening
NOV	/		
DEC	/		

CORIANDER
Coriandrum sativum

FEATURES

Also known as Chinese parsley or cilantro, this very quick-growing, bright green hardy annual reaches a height of approximately 60cm (24in). The leaves on the lower part of the stem are oval with serrated edges but as they mature on the outside branches they become feathery and are divided into narrow segments. The small flowers are white to pink, mauve or reddish and are borne in short-stalked clusters in summer. The spherical seeds are brownish yellow in colour, about 3mm (0.125in) in diameter and have a musty odour.

CONDITIONS

Aspect   Prefers a sunny position, sheltered from strong winds which could damage the plant.

Site   Grow in light, moderately rich, well-drained soil. Coriander is a fast-growing but short-lived herb which will grow in most soils that are not over-rich. Too much nitrogen lessens the flavour in the plant.

GROWING METHOD

Sowing and planting   Grow from seed sown from spring to autumn in the position it is to grow. (Sowing in seed trays is not advised as the young plants do not transplant well.) Successive sowings of seed several weeks apart will extend the cropping period. Plants from autumn sowings may need cloche protection. Sow directly into garden beds, into drills 13mm (0.5in) deep and 20cm (8in) apart. Seedlings appear within 1–2 weeks, two from each seed. Thin plants to 10–15cm (4–6in) apart.

Feeding   Water evenly and do not let the soil dry out. No fertiliser is necessary.

Problems   Usually free of pests, but may be attacked by greenfly. Hosing may damage the plants, so

GROWN AND MUCH LIKED by the ancient Egyptians, Babylonians and Greeks, coriander is also featured in Indian cookery.

wash the fly off gently or use liquid horticultural soap.

HARVESTING

Picking   Pick fresh leaves as required; the smaller immature leaves having the better taste. Harvest seed when leaves and flowers turn brown and the seed is ripe. Put seedheads upside down in a paper bag and hang it in a cool, dry, airy space. The ripened seeds should fall into the bag. Dig up roots in autumn.

Storage   Seeds are dried and stored in sealed jars or ground to a powder. The leaves cannot be dried satisfactorily.

Freezing   Leaves can be frozen for up to six months.

USES

Culinary   Leaves, seeds and roots are used for culinary purposes, especially in Asian cuisines. Both leaves and roots can be eaten fresh, the leaves having a pronounced sage flavour with citrus overtones and the roots having an additional nutty flavour. Ground coriander seed is much favoured as a spice.

Medicinal   Coriander is good for the digestive system.

CORIANDER AT A GLANCE

A quick-growing annual. Leaves and seeds are popular in cooking, especially in Asian cuisine. Hardy to minus 10 to minus 15°C.

			PARTS USED
JAN	/		
FEB	/		Leaves
MAR	plant		Seeds
APR	plant		Roots
MAY	plant	harvest	
JUN	plant	harvest	*Uses*
JULY	plant	harvest	Culinary
AUG	plant	harvest	Medicinal
SEPT	plant	harvest	
OCT		harvest	
NOV	/		
DEC	/		

CURRY PLANT

Helichrysum italicum, syn. angustifolium

FEATURES

The curry plant, *Helichrysum italicum*, is a hardy, evergreen, bushy sub-shrub that grows to about 60cm (2ft) high. The narrow silver leaves are highly aromatic, with a strong smell of curry, which becomes stronger when the leaves are touched or after rain. Clusters of small, mustard-yellow flowers are produced in summer.

CONDITIONS

Aspect   Plant in a sunny position. Protect roots from frost in colder districts. The curry plant dislikes winter wet.

Site   A light, well-drained soil is essential. In wet winters, if the soil is not sufficiently free-draining, plants can be lifted and grown on under glass.

GROWING METHOD

Sowing and planting   The curry plant does not tend to set good seed and so it is best propagated from cuttings taken in summer or in early autumn. Insert the cuttings in pots of a gritty, soil-based compost and overwinter the cuttings in a cold frame or greenhouse. Plant out the rooted cuttings the following spring when danger of hard frosts has passed.

Feeding   Water plants only in dry conditions. The curry plant will not tolerate conditions that are too wet. If your garden has wet clay soil, grow your curry plants in pots. Mulch helichrysums lightly in spring and autumn and give an application of a balanced general fertiliser in early spring.

Problems   The curry plant is not attacked by any particular pests or diseases.

Pruning   Trim established plants in the spring to maintain a neat shape, to remove winter-

THE SILVERY LEAVES of the curry plant make it an attractive garden plant, useful for hedging and edging

damaged shoots and to promote new growth. Lightly trim back after flowering to maintain shape and to prevent the plant from becoming too straggly.

HARVESTING

Picking   Pick leaves to use fresh or for drying at any time. Pick the flowers only when they are fully open.

Storage   Dry by hanging small bunches upside down in a cool, airy place. Store in dark, airtight, glass jars.

Freezing   Not suitable for freezing.

USES

Culinary   The leaves smell stronger than they taste, but sprigs can be added to chicken, vegetables, rice, etc. As the sprigs are woody they should be removed before serving.

Craft   Dried leaves and flowers can be added to spicy pot-pourri mixes and the flowers can be used for winter floral decorations.

Gardening   The bright silvery leaves make the curry plant a decorative garden plant, and it is sometimes used as hedging (position the plants 60cm (2ft) apart). The dwarf form (*Helichrysum microphyllum* or 'Nanum') is a more compact plant, reaching 30cm (1ft) in height and is also ideal for hedges and knot gardens (position the plants 30cm (1ft) apart).

CURRY PLANT AT A GLANCE

A bushy shrub with bright silvery leaves with a powerful scent of curry, but only a mild flavour. Hardy to minus 5 to minus 10°C.

JAN		harvest	*Parts used*
FEB		harvest	Leaves
MAR		harvest	Flowers
APR	plant	harvest	Sprigs
MAY	plant	harvest	
JUN	plant	harvest	
JULY	plant	harvest	*Uses*
AUG	plant	harvest	Culinary
SEPT	plant	harvest	Craft
OCT		harvest	Gardening
NOV		harvest	
DEC		harvest	

DANDELION
Taraxacum officinale

FEATURES

A perennial flower often seen as a weed in lawns or neglected places, dandelion produces a flat rosette of deeply lobed, bright green leaves from a big, fleshy taproot. Bright yellow flowers are produced in spring and summer on hollow, leafless stems and develop into puffy, spherical seedheads – dandelion clocks – the individual seeds of which float away on the breeze when ripe. Dandelion has a milky sap and its hollow flower stems differentiate it from other similar weeds, such as hieraciums.

CONDITIONS

Aspect Grows best in full sun.
Site Not fussy as to soil but you will get the biggest and best roots and less bitter leaves by growing it in good quality, friable soil.

GROWING METHOD

Sowing and planting Considered a weed in most gardens, the problem is usually restricting or removing it rather than growing it. Remove flowerheads before it sets seed. It is difficult to dig out as any bit of root left will regrow. It is best grown in a bottomless container to confine the roots. Although it is perennial, for the best crops dig out the mature plants each spring or two and replant from small pieces of root.
Feeding Keep the soil evenly moist. Avoid excessive fertilising. If the bed had well-rotted manure dug into it, no further fertilising is required. For container growth, incorporate controlled-release fertiliser into the potting mix at planting time and feed the growing plants monthly with liquid fertiliser.
Problems No particular problems.
Pruning Remove flower stems as they rise or, if the pretty flowers are wanted, deadhead as they

DANDELIONS are often considered a weed, but the yellow flowers are very pretty and the leaves are full of vitamins.

fade to stop unwanted seed formation. If seedheads are allowed to ripen, dandelion becomes an invasive weed.

HARVESTING

Picking Fresh spring leaves can be picked while small and sweet. Bigger, older leaves are very bitter. Bitterness can be reduced by blanching, that is, excluding light. Do this by covering the plant with an upturned tin or flower pot, being sure that all holes are covered. The leaves are ready for picking when they have lost all or most of their green colour. Harvest roots only in late autumn or winter or they will lack flavour and body. Pick flowers as they open for use fresh.
Storage Leaves and flowers must be used fresh but roots are stored by first roasting and grinding them and storing in an airtight jar.
Freezing Roasted, ground roots will stay fresher and more flavoursome if stored in the freezer.

USES

Culinary Young, sweet leaves are highly nutritious and can be used in salads, stir frys or to make teas. The ground roots are used as a coffee substitute. The flowers are used to make wine.
Medicinal The sticky, white sap of the dandelion is used to treat warts and verrucas. Dandelion coffee is sleep inducing and a detoxicant said to be good for the kidneys and liver. The leaves are a powerful diuretic.
Cosmetic Eating the leaves is said to be good for the skin.
Craft A yellow-brown dye is made from the roots.

DANDELION AT A GLANCE

This familiar 'weed' with its yellow flowers and 'dandelion clock' seedheads has many herbal uses. Hardy to minus 15°C or below.

JAN	/	
FEB	/	
MAR	plant 🌱	
APR	plant 🌱	harvest 🖐
MAY	plant 🌱	harvest 🖐
JUN		harvest 🖐
JULY		harvest 🖐
AUG		harvest 🖐
SEPT	plant 🌱	harvest 🖐
OCT		harvest 🖐
NOV	/	
DEC	/	

Parts used
Leaves
Flowers
Roots

Uses
Culinary
Medicinal
Cosmetic
Craft

DILL
Anethum graveolens

FEATURES

A hardy annual herb growing to 60–90cm (2–3ft), dill looks very like fennel, with its threadlike, feathery, aromatic, blue-green leaves. It has a single, thin taproot rising above the ground to form a long, hollow stalk. This stalk branches at the top to support a 15cm (6in) wide mass of small, yellow flowers, appearing in clusters, in summer. Flat, oval seeds, brown in colour, are produced quickly and in great quantities.

CONDITIONS

Aspect Prefers full sun. May need support and protection from strong winds.

Site Light, free-draining but fertile soils. Will not do well in cold, wet conditions.

GROWING METHOD

Sowing and planting Sow seed from spring to autumn. Successive planting every fortnight is recommended to ensure that there is continuous cropping. Sow the seeds in shallow furrows, with at least 60cm (2ft) between the rows, and then thin the seedlings out to 30cm (1ft) apart when they have reached approximately 5cm (2in) in height. Dill will quite often self-sow, so choose a permanent position for the initial plantings.

Feeding Keep well watered, especially in hot weather. Mulch well throughout spring and summer with well-rotted organic matter such as compost or farmyard manure.

Problems No particular problems.

HARVESTING

Picking Dill leaves can be picked within 2 months of

THE FEATHERY LEAVES and greenish-yellow flowers of dill make a graceful summer picture. The flowers are used in making spiced olives.

planting. Clip close to the stem in the cooler parts of the day. Several weeks after the plant blossoms, pick the flowerheads and place them in a paper bag – store in a cool, dry place until seeds ripen – or stems can be cut and hung upside down until seeds ripen and fall.

Storage Leaves and stems do not keep for more than a couple of days in the refrigerator before drooping and losing flavour. Dry leaves by spreading them thinly over a firm, non-metallic surface in a warm, dark place. After drying, place them in an airtight container. Seeds are dried in a similar manner.

Freezing Leaves and stems can be frozen for up to six months, and pieces broken off as required.

USES

Culinary Dill has a pronounced tang which is stronger in seed than leaf. Fresh leaves are used in many dishes, and as a garnish. The seeds are used ground or whole in cooked dishes, as well as in the making of vinegars, pickles and herb butters. Dried leaves are often added to soups or sauces. Dill is a great favourite in fish dishes. Tea can be made from the seeds.

Medicinal Dill was traditionally an important medicinal herb for coughs, headaches, digestive problems etc, and dill water or 'gripe water' is still used.

Gardening Dill is considered an ideal companion plant for lettuce, cabbage and onions.

DILL AT A GLANCE

A hardy annual with feathery blue-green leaves. Leaves and seeds are popular in cooking. Fairly hardy to about 0°C to minus 10°C.

		PARTS USED
JAN	/	
FEB	/	Leaves
MAR	plant 🌱	Seeds
APR	plant 🌱	Stems
MAY	plant 🌱 harvest 🌿	
JUN	plant 🌱 harvest 🌿	*Uses*
JULY	plant 🌱 harvest 🌿	Culinary
AUG	plant 🌱 harvest 🌿	Medicinal
SEPT	plant 🌱 harvest 🌿	Gardening
OCT	harvest 🌿	
NOV	/	
DEC	/	

ELDER
Sambucus nigra

FEATURES

A deciduous shrub or small tree, elder or elderberry grows up to 6–8m (20–28ft) tall and has rough, corky bark and compound leaves composed of five or so toothed, dark green leaflets. Heads of creamy white, scented flowers appear in summer leading to shiny, blue-black berries in autumn. The flowers attract bees while the berries are eaten by birds.

CONDITIONS

Aspect   A sunny position is best although the plant will tolerate bright, dappled shade or a few hours of full shade each day.

Site   Friable, fertile soil that drains well yet stays moist is best, but elder accepts a wide range of soil types. Grows well on chalky soils.

GROWING METHOD

Sowing and planting   Plants can be grown from seed sown in spring, or suckers, with their own roots, can be dug and detached from the parent plant. This can be done at any time but spring is best. Elders can also be propagated by cuttings. Take hardwood cuttings in late summer or tip cuttings in spring. Root in containers of very sandy potting mix. Pot up and overwinter under glass before planting out into their permanent position. If you are planting a group or row, leave at least 3m (10ft) between plants to allow room for the suckers to develop.

Feeding   Elders like moisture at their roots at all times, especially in hot, dry weather in summer. If rainfall is reliable and reasonably regular, mature plants usually need little extra water. In average garden soils no special fertilising is required, especially if you mulch beneath the plants with well-rotted organic matter. If soil is not particularly fertile, a ration of a complete

THE CREAMY-WHITE FLOWERS of the elder are strongly scented. They appear in clusters during early summer.

plant food once in early spring is sufficient.

Problems   No particular problems.

Pruning   Elder grows rapidly and in smaller gardens may need to be cut hard back in late autumn or early spring to prevent it growing too large.

HARVESTING

Picking   Flowerheads are picked in the morning but only when all the flowers on each head have bloomed. Dry spread out on a fine net in a cool, dark, airy place. Berries are picked when ripe.

Storage   Dried flowers can be removed from their stems and stored in airtight containers. Ripe berries can also be dried and similarly stored.

Freezing   Berries that have been cooked for a few minutes may be frozen for later use.

USES

Culinary   Fresh flowers are made into elderflower wine and cordials, and jams and jellies. The berries can also be made into jams or jellies and the juice can be fermented into elderberry wine. Berries should not be eaten raw.

Cosmetic   Cold elderflower tea splashed onto the face daily tones and soothes the skin and is good for the complexion generally. Leaves can also be used to make a soothing, healing wash.

Medicinal   An infusion of flowers is a remedy for respiratory problems, fevers, colds and sore throats and has a mild laxative effect. Berries are a mild laxative and are also used to treat coughs, colds, bronchitis, etc.

Gardening   Elderberries, with their dense growth and suckering habit, make a good privacy screen and reasonable windbreak.

ELDER AT A GLANCE

Deciduous tree with aromatic white flowers and purple berries, with many different uses. Hardy to minus 15°C or below.

JAN	/	*Parts used*	
FEB	/	Flowers	
MAR	/	Berries	
APR	plant	Leaves	
MAY	plant harvest		
JUN	harvest	*Uses*	
JULY	/	Culinary	
AUG	/	Medicinal	
SEPT	plant harvest	Cosmetic	
OCT	plant harvest	Gardening	
NOV	/		
DEC	/		

FENNEL
Foeniculum vulgare

FEATURES

Fast growing and spreading, this herbaceous perennial can reach 1.5–2.1m (5–7ft). An erect, finely foliaged plant with a strong aniseed aroma, it has a bulbous, fleshy base, hollow stems and delicate, thread-like, dark olive green leaves. Flattened heads of tiny, bright yellow flowers appear on the top of the plant in summer, followed by aromatic seeds. Fennel will self-seed very freely. 'Purpureum' is an attractive bronze-leaved cultivar. Florence fennel (*F. v.* var. *dulce*) is grown as an annual and the bulbous base of the stem is used as a vegetable.

CONDITIONS

Aspect Fennel prefers a sunny, sheltered position.
Site Grows on a wide variety of soils but is most vigorous on fertile, well-drained loamy soils. On acid soils, dig in a cupful of lime per square metre before planting as fennel prefers slightly alkaline conditions.

GROWING METHOD

Sowing and planting Most easily grown from seed sown in spring. Sow the seeds directly where they are to grow. Fennel will self-seed very freely and unwanted seedlings should be pulled out as early as possible, as they can be difficult to remove once the tough taproot is established. Fennel can also be propagated by division in autumn.
Feeding Keep well watered during spring and summer. Consistent moisture around the roots ensures sweet, succulent growth. Additional feeding is not necessary if the soil is rich and fertile. If in doubt, give an application of a balanced general fertiliser once in early spring.
Problems No particular problems.

FENNEL AT A GLANCE

Tall perennial with feathery aromatic foliage and aromatic seeds which are good for the digestion. Hardy to minus 15°C or below.

JAN	/	*Parts used*	
FEB	/	Leaves	
MAR	plant 🖐	Seeds	
APR	plant 🖐	Stems	
MAY	plant 🖐 harvest 🌾		
JUN	plant 🖐 harvest 🌾	*Uses*	
JULY	harvest 🌾	Culinary	
AUG	plant 🖐 harvest 🌾	Medicinal	
SEPT	plant 🖐 harvest 🌾	Cosmetic	
OCT	plant 🖐 harvest 🌾		
NOV	/		
DEC	/		

VERSATILE FENNEL has many culinary uses: the fleshy base is eaten as a vegetable, and seeds and leaves add flavour to other dishes.

Pruning Remove flowerheads before seeds are set and to encourage leaf production. Cut back top growth in late autumn.

HARVESTING

Picking Pick leaves any time from late spring to late summer. Pick stems when young and tender. Seeds are harvested when ripe in late summer and as this time approaches, plants should be inspected regularly so that ripe seeds can be gathered before they start to fall.
Storage Dried seeds are stored in airtight jars. Use the leaves fresh as they lose flavour during drying.
Freezing Put small bunches of leaves in a freezer bag or foil and freeze for up to 6 months.

USES

Culinary Seeds, which are an aid to digestion, are chewed raw or used whole or ground in recipes. Finely chopped leaves are added to many dishes, notably fish and carbohydrates such as pasta and potatoes, and to vinegars. Tender young stems can be used in salads.
Medicinal All parts of fennel are said to be beneficial to the digestion, good for the eyes and a mild appetite suppressant. Tea made from the seeds is a mild laxative. Chewing the seeds freshens stale breath. *Caution:* do not take in large doses.
Cosmetic Cold tea made from the seeds is a refreshing facial rinse that is said to reduce wrinkles and tone the skin.

FEVERFEW

Tanacetum parthenium, syn. *Chrysanthemum parthenium*

FEATURES

A perennial flower, feverfew has aromatic, finely cut leaves and clusters of long-lasting small, white daisy-like flowers in summer. The plant is densely foliaged and grows about 60cm (2ft) tall. Leaves are usually a fresh, light green but a golden foliaged form, 'Aureum', is also sold. Pretty double-flowered forms are also available.

CONDITIONS

Aspect Prefers full sun or light shade. Plants may grow lax and flower poorly in areas that are too shady. The golden form may scorch in full sun.

Site Average, well-drained garden soil is all that is needed. In over-rich soils plants produce too much soft, leafy growth.

GROWING METHOD

Sowing and planting Easily grown from seed sown in early spring. Press seeds just beneath the surface where the plants are to grow. Established plants can be dug up in autumn and divided into several new plants. Each division should have its own roots and the divisions should be replanted immediately. Soft-tip cuttings taken in early summer will also root easily. Make cuttings about 7.5cm (3in) long and insert them into small pots of very sandy potting mix. Place in a warm but shady and sheltered spot and keep them moist. Roots should form in about 3 weeks.

Feeding Do not overwater. Feverfew does not thrive on neglect but does not need frequent watering. Overwet conditions will cause the plant to rot.
Mulch lightly in spring and autumn and apply a balanced general fertiliser in spring.

Problems No major problems.

Pruning Can be cut back after flowering to keep a compact shape and to minimise self-seeding.

HARVESTING

Picking All the upper parts of the plant are useful medicinally and whole plants may be harvested any time they are in full bloom. Fresh, young leaves can be harvested any time, but are best before the plant flowers. Do remember that plants need their leaves to live and you should grow enough plants so that picking is not concentrated on just one or two. Pick flowers just as they open.

Storage Dry upper parts, including leaves, stems and flowers, in a cool, dark, airy place. (Hang flowers upside down to dry.) When dry, coarsely chop and store in an airtight jar.

Freezing Freshly picked leaves can be wrapped in foil and frozen, for up to 6 months, for later use.

FOR THE HERB GARDEN, most people prefer this single, daisy-like feverfew but there is also a very pretty double white one.

USES

Medicinal Tea made from the dried upper parts is drunk to relieve indigestion and period pain. It has gained a reputation for the treatment of migraines. Eating one or two fresh leaves every day may help prevent the onset of migraines in sufferers but in some people this causes mouth ulcers.

Cosmetic Feverfew makes a useful moisturiser.

Craft Flower stems placed in linen closets will discourage moths. An infusion of the leaves makes a mild disinfectant.

Gardening Feverfew is attractive and gives a good display when plants are massed together or used to border paths. It is attractive to bees and is often planted near fruit trees to assist pollination.

FEVERFEW AT A GLANCE

Perennial herb with aromatic leaves and daisy-like flowers that has a reputation for treating migraines. Hardy to minus 15°C.

Month	Activity		Parts used
JAN	/		
FEB	/		*Parts used*
MAR	plant		Flowers
APR	plant		Leaves
MAY	plant	harvest	Stems
JUN	plant	harvest	
JULY		harvest	*Uses*
AUG		harvest	Medicinal
SEPT	plant	harvest	Cosmetic
OCT	/		Craft
NOV	/		Gardening
DEC	/		

GARLIC
Allium sativum

FEATURES

Garlic grows from a bulb that consists of several segments, the strongly aromatic cloves that have led to its widespread culinary use. This perennial plant also has a long list of medicinal uses. Its erect, grey-green leaves stand 40–60cm (16–24in) tall, sometimes taller. Nondescript white flowers appear in summer, after which the leaves die back and the plant enters its annual winter dormancy.

CONDITIONS

Aspect   Grow in full sun.
Site   Good drainage is essential but garlic grows in any crumbly, reasonably fertile soil. Dark, sandy loam with well-rotted organic matter and a cupful of lime per square metre is ideal.

GROWING METHOD

Sowing and planting   In autumn or early spring, break cloves from a fresh garlic. Push into soil that is well dug over and crumbly so that the pointy end is 2.5cm (1in) below the surface. Space cloves about 15cm (6in) apart, cover with soil and water in well. Mulch lightly with compost or well-rotted manure.

Feeding   Newly planted garlic needs moisture for its developing roots but does not want to be sodden during autumn and winter. If rain does not fall, water deeply once a week. Gradually reduce watering as the weather warms up in spring as garlic needs a hot, dry summer to mature the bulbs. If garlic is grown in deep, fertile soil, an application of complete plant food at planting time is all the fertiliser needed.

Problems   Garlic can suffer from white rot. Remove affected plants and do not grow garlic in the same ground again.

GARLIC AT A GLANCE

Well known and widely used in cooking, garlic grows from a bulb made up of several cloves. Hardy to minus 15°C or below.

JAN	/		
FEB	plant 🖐		*Parts used*
MAR	plant 🖐		Cloves
APR	plant 🖐		Leaves
MAY	/		
JUN		harvest 🌿	*Uses*
JULY		harvest 🌿	Culinary
AUG		harvest 🌿	Medicinal
SEPT	plant 🖐	harvest 🌿	Gardening
OCT	plant 🖐	harvest 🌿	
NOV	/		
DEC	/		

THE PRINCE OF SEASONERS, garlic has a long history of use in medicine and magic, especially as protection against witchcraft.

HARVESTING

Picking   Harvest garlic in autumn or summer when the leaves have yellowed and died down. Do not cut the dead leaves off, but use them to plait the bulbs together for storage. After harvest, clean the bulbs and then leave in the sun for a few days to dry. Pick the fresh leaves as needed.

Storage   Dried bulbs may be strung together and hung in a dry, airy place for use as needed.

Freezing   Not suitable for freezing.

USES

Culinary   Garlic has hundreds of uses in virtually every type of cuisine. It is an essential ingredient in many European and Asian dishes, and it is used in vinegars, oils and herb butters. The leaves can be chopped and used in salads or lightly stir fried.

Medicinal   Garlic has strong antibiotic and antiseptic properties and is one of the most widely taken medicinal herbs. It is useful in lowering both blood pressure and cholesterol and it is said to have beneficial effects on the immune system. Regular intake of garlic will reduce susceptibility to colds and improve the digestive system. A sliced clove rubbed over cuts will clean and sterilise the wound. A sliced clove can also be rubbed over insect bites, boils, etc, but too much may cause an allergic skin reaction.

Gardening   Garlic is often planted under rose bushes as it is believed that it will not only improve their growth but also help to deter aphids and other rose pests.

HERB ROBERT
Geranium robertianum

FEATURES

A biennial herb, often grown as an annual, herb Robert may reach a height of 30–45cm (12–18in). It has deeply lobed, toothed leaves which sometimes develop a reddish cast. Pinkish flowers appear in spring in airy clusters. In the wild, the plant is widely distributed in temperate parts of the northern hemisphere. Explosive seed capsules make the plant potentially invasive where the conditions suit it.

CONDITIONS

Aspect   Full sun or part shade are equally suitable.
Site   Not particularly fussy about soil types as long as they drain freely. Average garden soil is quite satisfactory.

GROWING METHOD

Sowing and planting   Herb Robert can be grown from seed saved from last year and sown shallowly in spring or from cuttings of basal shoots taken in middle to late spring. Make cuttings about 7.5cm (3in) long and insert them into small pots of very sandy potting mix. Keep lightly moist in a warm, bright, but shaded place. Roots should form within a month and the new plants can either be placed in the garden or potted up to grow bigger. Herb Robert will self-seed freely and is considered to be a weed by many gardeners.

Feeding   Herb Robert does not need a lot of water and in places where summers are mild regular rainfall can be sufficient. If watering is necessary, water deeply once a week rather than giving more frequent light sprinklings. In garden beds that are mulched regularly with well-rotted organic matter, no further fertiliser is needed.

HERB ROBERT AT A GLANCE

Traditionally used as a medicinal herb, herb Robert is now often considered a weed. Hardy to minus 15°C or below.

JAN	/	*Parts used*	
FEB	plant	Leaves	
MAR	plant		
APR	plant		
MAY	plant harvest	*Uses*	
JUN	harvest	Medicinal	
JULY	harvest	Gardening	
AUG	harvest		
SEPT	harvest		
OCT	/		
NOV	/		
DEC	/		

HERB ROBERT has one of those scents you either like or loathe. It is said to be named after St Robert who discovered its medicinal qualities.

Problems   The fungus disease rust, which attacks all plants of the *Geranium* and *Pelargonium* genera, can disfigure the foliage and weaken the plant. It appears as yellow spots on the upper surface of the leaf with raised lumps of 'rust' underneath. Rust occurs mainly during warm, humid weather. To control it, either pick off affected leaves at the first sign of infection or spray the plant with a fungicide suitable for the condition (the label will tell you). Don't drop or compost any of the affected leaves. They should be burnt or placed into the rubbish bin.

HARVESTING

Picking   Leaves are used fresh and may be picked at any time as required.
Storage   Not usually stored.
Freezing   Not suitable for freezing.

USES

Medicinal   Traditionally, herb Robert has been used to treat a range of complaints as varied as toothache and conjunctivitis. *Caution:* do not use without expert supervision.
Gardening   Herb Robert plant is pretty enough in its own right and makes a good addition to a wild garden.

HOREHOUND

Marrubium vulgare

FEATURES

From the Mediterranean region, horehound, also known as white horehound, is a perennial with sprawling branches. It grows to a height of around 45cm (18in), sometimes more. The rough-textured, grey-green leaves are roundish and somewhat downy, especially when young. They have a strong aroma and are very bitter to taste. Dense, spherical heads of white flowers appear in summer and after blooming these dry to become stiff and spiky. Horehound will self-seed freely and can become a nuisance if not controlled.

CONDITIONS

Aspect Grow in full sun or part shade in a sheltered site.

Site Grows in a wide range of soil types if drainage is good. Plants rot if soil stays wet in winter.

GROWING METHOD

Sowing and planting Most easily raised from softwood cuttings taken from new growth in summer. Root the cuttings in pots of sandy potting mix kept shaded and moist. Mature, well-established plants may be dug up in late winter and divided into several smaller plants. Seeds saved from last year's flowers can also be used to start the plant. Sow them from middle to late spring where they are to grow. Thin seedlings to about 30cm (1ft) apart.

Feeding Horehound does best in a free-draining, dryish soil, and it can rot off if too wet, so be careful to avoid overwatering. Plants occur naturally in areas with dry, poor soils and in average garden conditions will not need any additional fertiliser. In poor soils, mulch in spring and autumn and apply a balanced general fertiliser in spring.

Problems No particular problems as far as pests or diseases are concerned but the plant can be spread widely by seed. Prevent this by removing the flowerheads immediately after they have finished blooming.

Pruning If plants are looking tattered by the end of autumn they may be cut to ground level. New growth will appear in spring.

HARVESTING

Picking Leaves to be used fresh can be picked at any time, but are best picked in late spring as the plants are about to come into flowers as this is when the oils are richest. Stems of flowers and leaves that are to be dried should be picked in the morning.

Storage Stems of dried flowers and leaves can be stored in airtight jars. Tie bunches of flowers and leaves together and hang them upside down in a dry, airy place. When they are dry, crumble into containers.

Freezing Not suitable for freezing.

HOREHOUND has been used to alleviate coughs and colds since the days of the ancient Egyptians. It has a place in any historical garden.

USES

Culinary Leaves can be boiled with sugar and water to make candied horehound, and they can also be used to give a bitter flavour to homebrew beer.

Medicinal Horehound tea, an infusion made from the leaves, stems and flowers, is taken for sore throats, coughs and colds and as a gentle laxative. Horehound is a diuretic and may be taken to help relieve kidney problems.

HOREHOUND AT A GLANCE

Sprawling perennial with woolly grey-green leaves. Traditionally used to treat coughs and colds. Hardy to minus 15°C or below.

JAN	/	
FEB	/	
MAR	plant	
APR	plant	
MAY	plant	harvest
JUN	plant	harvest
JULY		harvest
AUG		harvest
SEPT	plant	harvest
OCT	/	
NOV	/	
DEC	/	

Parts used
Leaves
Stems
Flowers

Uses
Culinary
Medicinal

HORSERADISH
Armoracia rusticana

FEATURES

Although it is a perennial plant, horseradish is also grown as an annual. It is a rather weedy looking plant, consisting as it does of a clump of big, soft, spinach-like leaves, and it is best grown tucked away in a corner of the vegetable patch. In some years a stem of unremarkable, off-white flowers rises from the centre of the clump in late summer. Horseradish can be invasive. The spreading roots are best confined by sinking stone slabs vertically into the soil to provide a physical barrier.

CONDITIONS

Aspect Horseradish prefers a sunny site but tolerates dappled shade.

Site Grow in deep soil that has been dug over deeply, a vegetable patch is ideal. This plant enjoys good conditions and thrives in well-drained soils that are rich in organic matter.

GROWING METHOD

Sowing and planting The entire root system may be dug up in late autumn and replanted in spring to control the plant's ability to spread rapidly. New plants are introduced into the garden as root cuttings. In early spring or autumn take 15cm (6in) cuttings of the straight, thin side-roots. These may be replanted immediately (allowing about 30cm (12in) between each plant) or started off in individual pots.

Feeding Keep horseradish moist during spring and summer. If grown in the vegetable patch, give it the same watering as other vegetables. Mix a ration of low nitrogen fertiliser into the planting hole and drench two or three times during the growing season with a high phosphate liquid plant food. Too much nitrogen makes too many leaves and poor quality roots.

Problems Snails, slugs and caterpillars are all drawn to the fleshy leaves and can strip young plants.

HARVESTING

Picking Main harvest is in autumn although side-roots can be snipped off in summer for immediate use. Do this by scraping soil away from the main root, replacing it when the desired roots have been cut. For the main harvest, lift the plant, ensuring that all roots are removed (or the plant will regrow). Use selected side-roots for regeneration, the rest for processing.

Storage Fresh whole roots can be stored in the refrigerator for about two weeks while the grated roots can be made into horseradish sauce or pickled in vinegar.

Freezing Whole roots can be wrapped in foil and frozen for up to 6 months.

HORSERADISH ROOTS are made into a piquant sauce for roast beef. In France they are sometimes eaten raw to stimulate the appetite.

USES

Culinary Horseradish sauce is a popular condiment with beef but can also be served with other meats and fish. It can be added sparingly to sauces and salad dressings.

Medicinal Horseradish aids digestion and is an instant remedy for blocked noses. It has antiseptic properties and is said to ward off colds if small amounts are eaten regularly. It is highly nutritious, containing high amounts of vitamin C and many essential minerals. It is a powerful circulatory stimulant. Grated into a poultice, it can be used for chilblains, stiff muscles, rheumatic joints etc, but overuse can cause the skin to blister. *Caution:* do not take more than very small amounts if pregnant or suffering kidney or thyroid problems.

HORSERADISH AT A GLANCE

A perennial with large spinach-like leaves, grown for its roots from which horseradish sauce is made. Hardy to minus 15°C.

JAN	/		*Parts used*	
FEB	/		Roots	
MAR	plant			
APR	plant			
MAY	plant		*Uses*	
JUN	/		Culinary	
JULY	/		Medicinal	
AUG		harvest		
SEPT	plant	harvest		
OCT	plant	harvest		
NOV		harvest		
DEC	/			

HYSSOP
Hyssopus officinalis

FEATURES

A semi-evergreen sub-shrub growing 60–80cm (24–32in) tall, hyssop has many erect stems clothed in narrow, lanceolate, sage green leaves. Spikes of small flowers appear on top of each stem in summer. Usually these flowers are blue-violet but they may also be pink or white. The whole plant exudes a pungent aroma and the leaves have a bitter taste.

CONDITIONS

Aspect Full sun produces compact growth and the strongest flavour but hyssop tolerates shade for part of the day.

Site Likes light, fertile, well-drained soils but will grow in any reasonably fertile soil as long as it drains freely.

GROWING METHOD

Sowing and planting Hyssop can be grown from seed, softwood cuttings or division of the roots. Sow seeds in spring in trays of seed compost. Cover lightly, keep moist and when seedlings are big enough to handle prick out into small, individual pots to grow on. Plant out about 30cm (12in) apart when plants are about 20cm (8in) tall. Take 7.5cm (3in) cuttings in early summer and insert into pots of sandy potting mix. Keep moist and in bright, sheltered shade and roots will form within a month. To divide, lift an established plant in late autumn or early spring. Cut the root mass into several smaller sections, each with its own roots. Replant immediately.

Feeding Keep soil moist, especially during the warmer months but do not overwater. Hyssop is a resilient plant that can often get by on rain. A ration of balanced general fertiliser in spring when new growth appears is enough.

Problems No particular problems.

HYSSOP AT A GLANCE

A decorative semi-evergreen shrub with narrow green leaves and spikes of blue flowers. Hardy to minus 15°C or below.

JAN	/	*Parts used*	
FEB	/	Leaves	
MAR	plant 🌱	Stems	
APR	plant 🌱	Flowers	
MAY	plant 🌱 harvest 🌾		
JUN	plant 🌱 harvest 🌾	*Uses*	
JULY	harvest 🌾	Culinary	
AUG	harvest 🌾	Medicinal	
SEPT	plant 🌱 harvest 🌾	Cosmetic	
OCT	plant 🌱	Gardening	
NOV	/		
DEC	/		

THE RICH BLUE FLOWERS of hyssop adorn the garden in spring, and they are much loved by bees who make superb honey from them.

Pruning When new growth begins in spring, pinching out the tips of young stems will encourage the plant to become more bushy and thus produce more flowers. Trim after flowering to maintain shape.

HARVESTING

Picking Flowers for using fresh or for drying are picked when in full bloom and individual stems can be harvested as needed.

Storage Cut bunches of flowering stems, tie them together and hang them upside down in a dim, airy place. When they are dry, crumble them into airtight jars.

Freezing Not suitable for freezing.

USES

Culinary One or two fresh leaves, finely chopped and added late, give an appealing piquancy to soups and casseroles while fresh flowers can be used to add flavour and colour to salads.

Medicinal Tea, made by infusing the dried stems, leaves and flowers in boiling water, is taken to relieve the symptoms of colds; hyssop leaves are often a component in mixed herbal tonics and teas. *Caution:* do not use during pregnancy or for nervous people. Avoid strong doses and do not use continuously for long periods.

Cosmetic Oil distilled from hyssop is used in perfumes and other commercial cosmetics. At home, it may be added to bath water, and cooled hyssop leaf tea is a cleansing, refreshing facial rinse.

Gardening Hyssop is a decorative plant and very attractive to bees and butterflies. Use it in a border of mixed flowers or grow it as an edging to paths.

LAVENDER
Lavandula

FEATURES

Lavender is a traditional herb and cottage garden plant. An evergreen, bushy shrub with aromatic, narrow, grey-green leaves, it bears spikes of blue-mauve (and in some varieties pink or white) fragrant flowers in summer. There are many species and varieties to choose from, most hardy but some only half hardy, and the fragrance and herbal properties will vary with the different types. Heights vary from 30cm (12in) to 80cm (32in) or more. 'Common' or 'English' lavender is *Lavandula angustifolia* (favourite varieties include 'Alba', 'Hidcote' and 'Munstead'). Popular half hardy lavenders include *L. dentata* and *L. stoechas*.

CONDITIONS

Aspect   Best grown in an open, sunny position, but will tolerate some shade. Lavender will not do well in cold, wet conditions.

Site   Prefers well-drained soil, but it need not be rich. If it is acid, add lime.

GROWING METHOD

Sowing and planting   Some lavenders will flower the first year from an early sowing, but taking cuttings is the easiest way to get the lavender you want. Take 5cm (2in) cuttings with a heel or base of old wood in summer. Trim off lower leaves and insert into pots of a sandy potting mix. Keep on the dry side until the cutting has taken root and new leaf shoots appear. Pot on into a good quality potting mix. Plant in the garden in spring 45–60cm (18–24in) apart. Layering is easily done in autumn with most hardy lavenders.

Feeding   Water only in dry weather as lavenders do not require a great deal of water. Applications of a balanced general fertiliser will improve fragrance. Less cold-resistant varieties may need winter mulching.

Problems   In wet conditions lavender may suffer from grey mould or botrytis. Remove and burn affected parts.

Pruning   Trim in spring and again after flowering to keep a compact shape and prevent the bush from becoming straggly. The final trim of the year should be well before the last frosts as frost will damage soft new growth. Do not cut back into old wood as this is unlikely to re-shoot.

HARVESTING

Picking   Flowers can be cut just as they open. Leaves can be picked at any time.

Storage   Dry by hanging in bunches in a dry, airy, hot place. Store dried leaves and flowers in airtight jars.

Freezing   Not suitable for freezing.

ENGLISH LAVENDER is distinguished from the dumpier French, Italian and Spanish types by its slender flower spikes.

USES

Culinary   Fresh or dried flowers and leaves are used to flavour sugars, jellies, ice creams and cheeses. Flowers can also be crystallised and used as decoration on cakes.

Medicinal   Lavender has traditionally had many medicinal uses, including soothing and sedating and healing burns, cuts and stings. The oil has a strong anti-bacterial action. It is also used to treat headaches.

Cosmetic Craft   Lavender is used to make skin and hair washes. Dried lavender spikes are used in pot-pourris, perfumed sachets and dried arrangements. Lavender is used to make essential oil and floral waters. It is also an insect repellent.

Gardening   Popular, widely grown cottage garden plants.

LAVENDER AT A GLANCE

Popular fragrant garden plants with narrow silvery leaves and strongly scented flowers. Hardiness varies: minus 5 to minus 15°C.

Month	Activity		*Parts used*
JAN	/		Flowers
FEB	/		Leaves
MAR	plant ✣		
APR	plant ✣		
MAY	plant ✣	harvest ✣	*Uses*
JUN	plant ✣	harvest ✣	Culinary
JULY	plant ✣	harvest ✣	Medicinal
AUG	plant ✣	harvest ✣	Cosmetic
SEPT	plant ✣	harvest ✣	Craft
OCT	/		Gardening
NOV	/		
DEC	/		

LEMON BALM

Melissa officinalis

FEATURES

A clump-forming perennial growing to 60–90cm (2–3ft) high, lemon balm, has small, serrated, nettle-like leaves with a strong lemon scent. They are supported on squarish stems with spikes of inconspicuous yellow-white flowers borne in the axils of the leaves during summer. These plants may die back during winter, but established plants will regenerate in spring. In its favoured soil conditions it can become invasive. Lemon balm is also known as bee balm because it is very attractive to bees. Attractive gold-leaved ('All Gold') and gold variegated ('Aurea' or 'Variegata') forms are available.

CONDITIONS

Aspect Will grow in full sun or partial shade.
Site Soils should be rich in organic matter and kept moist and well mulched.

GROWING METHOD

Sowing and planting Lemon balm can be propagated three ways. Sow seeds in early spring in seed trays, prick out in mid spring and plant out during late spring, 45cm (18in) apart. Seed can be slow to germinate, but self-sown seedlings can often be found around an existing plant. Root division of the parent plant in early spring or autumn is also successful. Replant immediately. Cuttings 10–12cm (4–6in) long can be taken from new spring growth.
Feeding Keep plants well watered in hot, dry spells. Apply a balanced general fertiliser once in early spring when new growth begins.
Problems Lemon balm may be affected by a rust disease. Cut the plant to the ground and dispose of all affected parts.
Pruning Keep straggly clumps in shape by pruning

ELIZABETHAN HOUSEWIVES used to rub furniture with sprigs of lemon balm to scent the wood. Bees love the tiny flowers.

during spring. This promotes further growth for summer. Top growth can be cut back to soil level in autumn.

HARVESTING

Picking Pick fresh leaves as required. Whole stems may be cut when flowers begin to emerge and then dried. Leaves are most tender and full of flavour in spring.
Storage Dry quickly by hanging cut stems in a cool, airy space. Rub dry leaves and flowers from the stems and store in airtight jars. However, lemon balm leaves are best used fresh as the aroma is rapidly lost when dried.
Freezing Put in freezer bag; freeze for up to 6 months.

USES

Culinary Fresh leaves and flowers are used in salads and the leaves are also used in stuffings or sauces for poultry and fish. Lemon balm herbal teas are very popular and fresh leaves can also be used to flavour cool summer drinks.
Medicinal Lemon balm tea relieves tension and headaches and is used to improve digestion and relieve colds and flu. Leaf poultices have been used to treat wounds, stings and insect bites.
Craft Lemon balm has traditionally been used to scent furniture polish.
Gardening Lemon balm is also known as bee balm and is particularly attractive to bees. It can be planted in orchards to attract pollinating bees. Plant it next to a path, and the powerful lemon scent will be released as you brush against it.

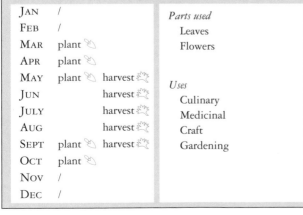

LEMON BALM AT A GLANCE

Clump-forming perennial with fresh green leaves that have a delicious lemon scent. Hardy to minus 15°C or below.

		Parts used
JAN	/	Leaves
FEB	/	Flowers
MAR	plant 🌱	
APR	plant 🌱	
MAY	plant 🌱 harvest 🌿	Uses
JUN	harvest 🌿	Culinary
JULY	harvest 🌿	Medicinal
AUG	harvest 🌿	Craft
SEPT	plant 🌱 harvest 🌿	Gardening
OCT	plant 🌱	
NOV	/	
DEC	/	

LEMON GRASS
Cymbopogon citratus

FEATURES

Also known as citronella grass, lemon grass is a tender perennial grass of tropical regions. The narrow, ribbon-like, leafy stalks grow in clumps that, in the right conditions, reach 90cm (3ft) or more in length. The leaves swell slightly at the base to form a fleshy stolon or underground stem. The stem is white and is also edible. Lemon grass rarely flowers.

CONDITIONS

Aspect   Lemon grass is best grown in a container in sun or partial shade, and brought in to be overwintered in a warm greenhouse or conservatory.

Site   Lemon grass requires rich, fertile soils. Use a good quality potting compost and feed regularly throughout the growing season. If growing lemon grass outdoors, incorporate plenty of organic matter in the form of compost, leaves, straw or well-rotted farmyard manure before planting, and mulch constantly throughout the growing season to retain moisture levels.

GROWING METHOD

Sowing and planting   Lemon grass rarely flowers. Root pieces of lemon grass bought from the supermarket or propagate mature plants in spring. To do this, divide the mature plant, breaking off portions from the outer edge of the clump, and then replant immediately.

Feeding   Water well as this plant requires a great deal of water, especially during the earlier stages of its growth. In spring and summer while the plant is growing strongly, apply liquid or soluble fertiliser monthly.

Problems   Lemon grass is not attacked by any particular pests or diseases.

LEMON GRASS is an untidy grower but it can be kept presentable by trimming the foliage back in spring. The flowers are unexciting.

HARVESTING

Picking   Pick leaves or remove portions of the stem in summer as required.

Storage   Harvested portions can be kept in the refrigerator for a few days. Lemon grass cannot be dried.

Freezing   Can be put in a freezer bag and frozen for up to 6 months.

USES

Culinary   Lemon grass is widely used in the cuisines of south-east Asia. The 'sweet-sour', lemony flavour of the leaves is used in making herbal teas. Pieces of lemon grass leaves can be tied together and used to flavour marinades. The leaves are also used in cooking in a variety of dishes. The white, fleshy stem of lemon grass is chopped and used to flavour a range of cooked dishes such as curries, fish or soups. The stem may be discarded after cooking. Lemon grass leaves can also be incorporated into fresh salads.

LEMON GRASS AT A GLANCE

A tender perennial from the tropics, it produces lemony-flavoured leaves, much used in Asian cuisine. Not hardy.

JAN	/	
FEB	/	
MAR	/	
APR	plant 🌱	
MAY	plant 🌱	
JUN		harvest 🌿
JULY		harvest 🌿
AUG		harvest 🌿
SEPT	/	
OCT	/	
NOV	/	
DEC	/	

Parts used
Leaves
Stem

Uses
Culinary

LEMON VERBENA
Aloysia triphylla, syn. *Lippia citriodora*

FEATURES

A large, bushy, deciduous shrub that grows 1–3m (3–10ft) in height, lemon verbena has long, lemony-scented, narrow leaves. Spikes or sprays of small white to mauve flowers appear in the axils of the leaves in summer. The leaves give this plant its herby quality, and their fragrance can be released simply by brushing against them in the garden. It can be grown in containers and in cooler areas brought indoors over winter, although container plants do not reach the same height as garden plants.

CONDITIONS

Aspect Requires a sheltered, sunny position with winter protection. Against a sunny wall is ideal.

Site Likes rich soils. Needs mulching against frosts.

GROWING METHOD

Sowing and planting Grow from softwood cuttings in late spring or hardwood cuttings in autumn. Trim a 12cm (5in) piece from the parent bush, removing a third of the upper leaves and a few of the lower leaves. Place in a sandy potting mix. Moisten the mix and cover the pot with a plastic bag to create a mini-greenhouse. Pot on into good quality potting compost when the cutting has taken root and shows renewed leaf growth. Plant in the garden when the plant is growing strongly.

Feeding The plant is tolerant of dry conditions and will rarely require watering except when grown in a pot. Mulch with straw in autumn to protect from frost. Give an application of a balanced general fertiliser in spring.

Problems Spider mite and whitefly can be a problem. Hose leaves frequently to remove the pests or use organic soap and pyrethrum or recommended chemicals.

THIS HERB was introduced to European gardens from Chile in 1746. The name Aloysia honours Queen Maria Louisa of Spain.

Pruning Prune each season to contain its straggly growth habit, and cut out frost-damaged shoots in spring. It can be trained into a formal standard.

HARVESTING

Picking Sprigs of leaves can be harvested at any time.

Storage Hang the branches in a cool, airy place and strip off the leaves when they are dry. Store dried leaves in airtight jars. Fragrance remains for some years.

Freezing Put in a freezer bag and freeze for up to 6 months.

USES

Culinary Fresh or dried leaves can be used for herbal tea or in cooking where a lemony flavour is required, as with fish, poultry, marinades, salad dressings and puddings, and to flavour oils and vinegars.

Medicinal Lemon verbena tea has a mild sedative effect and is good for nasal congestion and indigestion. *Caution:* long-term use may cause stomach irritation.

Cosmetic The leaves can be used in skin creams and the essential oil is used in perfumery.

Craft The strong long-lasting fragrance makes dried leaves a popular component of pot-pourris and sachet fillings.

Gardening Lemon verbena is an attractive border and container plant.

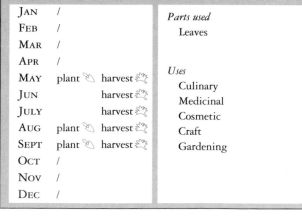

LEMON VERBENA AT A GLANCE

A deciduous shrub with lemon-scented leaves which are popular ingredients in pot-pourris and sachets. Hardy to minus 5°C.

JAN	/	
FEB	/	
MAR	/	
APR	/	
MAY	plant ✤ harvest ❧	*Parts used*
JUN	harvest ❧	Leaves
JULY	harvest ❧	
AUG	plant ✤ harvest ❧	*Uses*
SEPT	plant ✤ harvest ❧	Culinary
OCT	/	Medicinal
NOV	/	Cosmetic
DEC	/	Craft
		Gardening

LOVAGE
Levisticum officinale

FEATURES

A very tall perennial herb that reaches in excess of 2m (6.5ft), this plant looks quite spectacular when growing in the garden. Dark green to yellowish leaves become smaller towards the top of the plant and break into wedge-shaped, ridged leaflets. Greenish flowers appear in summer, and then are followed by small, light brown, grooved, aromatic seeds. The hollow, ribbed stems of lovage look and taste like celery and there is a longish tap root that is much like a carrot. Lovage dies back to ground level over winter but it will regenerate in the following spring.

CONDITIONS

Aspect   Lovage grows in full sun or semi-shade.
Site   Prefers moist, fertile, well-drained alkaline soil.

GROWING METHOD

Sowing and planting   Lovage is most easily propagated by seed, and self-sown seedlings will often be found around established plants. Sow seeds under glass in spring, or in the garden where they are to grow in autumn or spring. Plant out approximately 30cm (12in) apart. Mature plants of at least two seasons can be propagated by dividing the roots in autumn or spring.
Feeding   Water well, especially in hot, dry weather. Give an application of a balanced general fertiliser once in early spring.
Problems   Aphids love lovage and can transmit viral diseases to the plant. Hose vigorously to break their cycle or treat with organic or recommended insecticidal sprays. Leaf miner maggots will tunnel into leaves causing white blotches. Remove infected leaves.
Pruning   Prune flowers in summer for a bushier plant.

LOVAGE has been long grown and used in cooking: the ancient Roman writer Apicius featured its mild flavour in many of his recipes.

HARVESTING

Picking   Harvest leaves in early summer as they develop a more bitter flavour after flowering. Harvest seeds as they begin to turn brown. Pick heads on a dry day, put in a paper bag and hang in a dry airy place. Harvest stems any time. Dig roots in autumn when plants are 2-3 years old.
Storage Freezing   All parts can be dried and kept in airtight jars. Leaves can be blanched in boiling water and then quick frozen in small lots or frozen within ice cubes. Can be frozen for up to 6 months.

USES

Culinary   Leaves, stems and seeds are substitutes for celery. Try leaves and stems in fresh salads and dried seeds in soups, casseroles, sauces and pickling mixtures, or savoury biscuits, breads and pastries. Lovage is also used in teas, vinegars and butters.
Medicinal Traditionally used for digestive problems, rheumatism and to reduce water retention. *Caution:* do not use if pregnant or if you have kidney problems.
Cosmetic   Lovage is deodorising and antiseptic. A decoction can be added to bath water.

LOVAGE AT A GLANCE

A tall perennial herb with dark green leaves, used in cooking for its celery flavour. Hardy to minus 15°C or below.

JAN	/		*Parts used*	
FEB	/		Leaves	
MAR	plant		Stems	
APR	plant		Seeds	
MAY	plant	harvest	Roots	
JUN		harvest		
JULY		harvest	*Uses*	
AUG		harvest	Culinary	
SEPT	plant	harvest	Medicinal	
OCT	plant	harvest	Cosmetic	
NOV	/			
DEC	/			

MARJORAM

Origanum majorana, syn. *Majorana hortensis*

FEATURES

This variety of marjoram, known as sweet or knotted marjoram, is a tender, bushy perennial herb. It is usually grown as an annual as it does not survive cold winters. It can grow to 25–30cm (10–12in) or more, producing small, oval leaves covered with fine hair. The leaves are light green on top and grey-green underneath and are borne on short stalks. During summer very small, white to lilac flowers appear in clusters, from buds that resemble knots (hence the name), and later tiny, light brown seeds are produced.

CONDITIONS

Aspect Grow in full sun in a sheltered position.
Site Does best in quite rich soils that are well-drained and preferably alkaline. Add plenty of compost and well-rotted farmyard manure. Add lime if the soil is too acidic.

GROWING METHOD

Sowing and planting Seeds are slow to germinate and are usually sown indoors in trays. Pot on into small containers after the first few true leaves have formed, and then put into the garden in spring. Plant in small clumps 15cm (6in) apart. Propagation by cuttings is also possible, during late summer. Take a 7.5cm (3in) piece of woody stem from the parent plant, trim the leaves from the cutting and strike it in a mixture of two-thirds coarse sand to one-third compost. Transplant in spring when the root structure is established and new growth appears on the stem. Roots of a mature plant can also be divided in autumn.

Feeding Water adequately but do not overwater. Little additional fertiliser is needed in a good soil. If poor, apply liquid organic fertiliser or

THIS FAVOURITE HERB of Italian cookery was regarded by the Romans as sacred to Venus: they wore marjoram at their weddings.

seaweed-based conditioner every six weeks.

Problems Damping off of seedlings is one problem of this herb: they become water-soaked, shrivel and die. Keep seed beds warm and use good quality, sterile seed compost. Bad drainage will bring on this disease, and root rot in older plants. Pests include aphids and spider mite. Hose down, or treat with insecticide.

Pruning Flowers can be pruned at knot stage to maintain the shape of the bush. Trim after flowering to prevent plants becoming straggly.

HARVESTING

Picking Pick leaves to use fresh for culinary use at any time. Harvest leaves to be dried and unopened knot-like flowers in summer – the stems can be cut down to 5cm (2in) above the ground – and hang them to dry in a cool, shady spot.

Storage Remove leaves and buds from stems and store in airtight jars. Discard stems.

Freezing Chop finely, mix with a little water and freeze in ice cubes.

USES

Culinary The taste resembles that of a mild oregano and can be substituted for it. It is often used in the French bouquet garni. Fresh leaves and flowers can be used in salads, stuffings for meat and poultry, or in marinades. The flavour blends with most vegetable dishes and can also be used to flavour vinegars and oils. Dried, it makes a refreshing herbal tea.

Medicinal The teas is good for the digestion and for colds. An infusion in the bath aids relaxation.

Craft Marjoram adds fragrance in pot-pourris.

MARJORAM AT A GLANCE

Sweet marjoram is a tender bushy herb used in cooking for its mild oregano flavour. Hardy to about minus 5°C at best.

JAN	/	
FEB	/	
MAR	plant 🌱	
APR	plant 🌱	
MAY	plant 🌱	harvest 🌿
JUN		harvest 🌿
JULY		harvest 🌿
AUG	plant 🌱	harvest 🌿
SEPT	plant 🌱	harvest 🌿
OCT	/	
NOV	/	
DEC	/	

Parts used
Leaves
Flowers

Uses
Culinary
Medicinal
Craft

MINT
Mentha

MINT IS VERY INVASIVE, spreading rapidly by underground runners. If you cannot afford the space to give it its head, as here, it can be grown in a tub as long as you remember to keep it well watered. The prettily variegated apple mint is less rampant than the green-leaved kinds.

FEATURES

There are many varieties of mint, but all are perennials and they all have square stems and invasive, spreading roots. They can be prostrate or upright in nature. The simple, light to dark green or mottled leaves have toothed edges and their own individual fragrance, depending on variety. The small, flowers are purple, pink or white and are borne in whorls on terminal spikes. They appear in summer. Because of their invasive nature, mints are best grown in containers or in garden beds that have a solid border at least 50cm (20in) deep.

CONDITIONS

Aspect Mint prefers a semi-shaded position and can be grown indoors in a container. It will grow in full sun if the soil is kept moist.

Site Soil should be moderately rich, and well mulched so it retains moisture. The addition of too much organic matter or fresh manures to the bed will, however, encourage rust diseases.

GROWING METHOD

Sowing and planting Most mints can be raised from seed (although some varieties cannot be propagated this way),

MINTS AT A GLANCE

Spreading perennials. The leaves, which come in a range of flavours, are much used in cooking. Generally hardy to minus 15°C.

JAN	/	
FEB	/	
MAR	plant 🤚	
APR	plant 🤚	
MAY	plant 🤚	harvest 🍃
JUN	plant 🤚	harvest 🍃
JULY		harvest 🍃
AUG		harvest 🍃
SEPT		harvest 🍃
OCT	/	
NOV	/	
DEC	/	

Parts used
  Leaves

Uses
  Culinary
  Medicinal
  Gardening

ABOVE: The tiny Corsican mint is the most strongly scented and flavoured of all mints. It makes a delightful groundcover.

TOP LEFT: Spearmint is the most widely used type of mint and the one you will be offered at a nursery if you ask for 'mint'.

BOTTOM LEFT: Eau-de-cologne mint is rather bitter and must be used sparingly in cooking. It lends its scent to eau de cologne.

but this often gives inferior plants so mints are best propagated by root cuttings or division. Division during spring and summer is the easiest method of propagation. Lift runners, divide them and replant in rich, moist soil.

Feeding Keep soil moist as mint must always have plenty of water. Feeding is not necessary if mints are planted in well-mulched soil.

Problems Spider mite can be treated with an appropriate spray. Discolouring of leaves may indicate mint rust. Cut out any infected leaves and stems and put them in the bin. A form of wilt causes leaves to brown and drop. Treat the wilt by removing diseased plants and do not feed with high nitrogen fertilisers.

Pruning Frequent pruning of the stems forces lateral branching and healthier plants.

HARVESTING

Picking Young, fresh leaves can be picked at any time. The younger the leaf, the tenderer and tastier it will be.

Storage Leaves can be dried by placing them on a rack in a cool, airy space. When they are dry,

crumble them and store them in airtight jars.

Freezing Fresh leaves can be chopped and frozen in small packages or in ice cubes.

USES

Culinary Mints have a wide range of flavours from the fruity taste of apple mint to the perfume-like one of the eau-de-cologne variety, making them very useful, especially in sauces or jellies. They can be used fresh in salads, drinks, vinegars or as a garnish. Dried mints can be used in place of some of the salt in soups. Peppermint is used to make a popular herbal tea.

Medicinal Peppermint traditionally has a wide range of uses, from headaches and colds to digestive complaints. It is also said to improve concentration. An infusion can be used for a refreshing bath.

Gardening Some organic gardeners promote the growth of mint around apple trees to ward off moths, but there is some doubt about its effectiveness. Peppermint and spearmint are said to deter aphids if planted near roses.

NASTURTIUM
Tropaeolum majus

TROPAEOLUM means 'a little trophy', so named because the shield-shaped leaves and golden, helmet-like flowers suggested piles of armour.

FEATURES

A popular trailing garden plant. Compact varieties grow to about 60cm (24in) while large varieties can spread up to 3m (10ft). The wide leaves are roundish and dark green to variegated in colour and have a peppery taste. The funnel-shaped, five-petalled and spurred flowers appear in late spring and summer and range from creamy white through yellow to salmon, brilliant orange and red. Some varieties have double flowers and all have a slight perfume. Each bud produces a cluster of seeds. (Double forms do not produce seed.) This plant grows well in containers.

CONDITIONS

Aspect Prefers full sun although it will grow in semi-shade. Leaf growth is more pronounced in shady situations and may hide the blooms.

Site Nasturtiums do not like an over-rich soil but good drainage is necessary. Too rich a soil will encourage leaves at the expense of flowers.

GROWING METHOD

Sowing and planting For early flowers sow the large seeds under glass in spring. Plugs or small pots are ideal. Plant out 20cm (8in) apart when all danger of frost has passed. Seeds can be sown outdoors in May directly where they are to grow, but the plants will not flower until a few weeks later than the early sowings.

Feeding Do not water excessively, especially when plants are well established. Nitrogen encourages the growth of leaves. More flowers and seeds will be produced if you hold back on the fertiliser and compost.

Problems Sap-sucking blackfly (aphids) love nasturtiums. Vigorously hose the pest off or treat the plant with an appropriate spray. Caterpillars, particularly those of the cabbage white butterfly, can also be a problem.

HARVESTING

Picking Pick fresh leaves, buds and flowers as required. Harvest seeds just before they lose their green colour.

Storage Leaves and flowers do not store well and should be used immediately. Buds and seeds can be pickled in vinegar, stored in airtight jars and used at a later date.

Freezing Put in a freezer bag; freeze for up to 6 months.

USES

Culinary All parts of this herb are edible and have a spicy, peppery flavour. Fresh leaves and flowers are used in salads or the flowers can be used alone as a garnish. Buds and seeds are used as a substitute for capers. *Caution:* do not eat large quantities at one time.

Gardening Because they are so attractive to aphids, nasturtiums are excellent companion plants for vegetables such as cabbages, broccoli and other brassicas. The aphids will flock to the nasturtiums and leave the vegetables alone.

NASTURTIUM AT A GLANCE

Attractive trailing annuals with brightly coloured flowers, grown for decoration and for the kitchen. Hardy to minus 5°C.

			Parts used
JAN	/		Leaves
FEB	/		Flowers
MAR	plant ✑		Buds
APR	plant ✑		Seeds
MAY	plant ✑	harvest ✿	
JUN	plant ✑	harvest ✿	
JULY		harvest ✿	Uses
AUG		harvest ✿	Culinary
SEPT		harvest ✿	Gardening
OCT		harvest ✿	
NOV	/		
DEC	/		

OENOTHERA
Oenothera biennis

FEATURES

Oenothera, the evening primrose, is a hardy biennial with many upright, leafy stems. In summer each of these stems is topped with a cluster of golden yellow, sweetly fragrant flowers which open towards the end of the day. The scent is strongest in the evening. The foliage, which is bright green, forms a rosette around the base of the plant. Evening primrose should be planted with caution as it self-seeds prolifically and spreads fast in favoured locations.

CONDITIONS

Aspect Full sun is preferred.
Site Not very fussy about soil and grows in most places so long as the drainage is good. This plant thrives in average garden soils.

GROWING METHOD

Sowing and planting Grows from seed sown in autumn or early spring directly where it is to grow. Thin seedlings out so that there is at least 30cm (1ft) between them.
Feeding Do not overwater. Once established, plants are fairly drought tolerant. Feeding is not necessary. Rich soils can lead to excessive foliage growth and weak or deformed stems.
Problems No particular problems.
Pruning Pruning is not necessary. Snap off flower stems after the blooms have faded but before seeds ripen. This plant self-seeds freely and can create a major weed problem. Allow one plant to seed in order to regenerate the plants but collect the seed before it falls.

HARVESTING

Picking Leaves may be picked at any time, while seeds

EVENING PRIMROSE earns its name by blooming at dusk. There are perennial species that keep their blooms open all day.

are harvested when ripe in autumn. Pick flowers in bud or when just open. The small roots may also be dug in spring or autumn.
Storage Seeds are stored in airtight containers. Other parts of the plant are used fresh.
Freezing Not suitable for freezing.

USES

Culinary All parts of the plant are edible. Fresh leaves are used in salads or can be lightly steamed or stir fried. Seeds can be eaten raw or used in cooking.
Medicinal Tea made from the leaves is good for coughs and colds and is a tonic for the liver, kidneys and intestines. An oil (GLA, gamma linoleic acid) contained in the seeds has been credited with amazing therapeutic powers, and evening primrose is now being grown commercially on a large scale.
Gardening Evening primrose is a pretty plant and a good partner for other meadow flowers such as Californian poppies.

OENOTHERA AT A GLANCE

The evening primrose is a pretty, fragrant, yellow-flowered biennial, now much grown commercially. Hardy to minus 15°C.

JAN	/		
FEB	/		
MAR	plant 🌱		
APR	plant 🌱		
MAY	plant 🌱	harvest 🌾	
JUN	plant 🌱	harvest 🌾	
JULY		harvest 🌾	
AUG		harvest 🌾	
SEPT	plant 🌱	harvest 🌾	
OCT		harvest 🌾	
NOV	/		
DEC	/		

Parts used
Leaves
Stems
Flowers
Buds
Seeds
Roots

Uses
Culinary
Medicinal
Gardening

OREGANO
Origanum vulgare

FEATURES

Oregano is very closely related to marjoram and is often confused with it. Three varieties of this summer flowering perennial are widely grown. Common or wild oregano, *O. vulgare*, is a small shrub growing 30–45cm (12–18in) high, with woody stems and oval, soft, hairy leaves and tiny, white flowers. Golden oregano, *O. vulgare* 'Aureum', is very decorative in the garden; the leaves are golden-yellow in colour and the flowers are pink. Greek or white oregano, *O. vulgare* ssp. *hirsutum*, has dark green leaves covered with a white, hairy bloom and has a very pungent flavour. The flowers are white.

CONDITIONS

Aspect   Grow in full sun or partial shade, except for golden-leaved varieties which are best given some shade as the leaves may scorch in full sun.

Site   Likes well-drained, not too rich garden soil. Mulch to keep soils moist in hot, dry weather.

GROWING METHOD

Sowing and planting   Sow seeds in spring. Temperatures need to be above 20°C for the best results. Transplant seedlings into the garden when well established. More often, propagate by root division in late spring as it spreads by underground stems, or propagate by layering. Scarify the under-surface of the stem, peg it down and cover with soil. Keep damp until roots form, cut off and replant. Oregano can also be propagated by cuttings taken either in the spring or in summer. Replace the plants every couple of years as the stems become woody.

Feeding   Keep plants well watered, but do not allow the

GOLDEN-LEAVED OREGANO is more decorative than the ordinary green version and just as fine in flavour and scent.

soil to become waterlogged. Little additional feeding is needed if they are grown in well-mulched soil.

Problems   Aphids, leaf miner and spider mite should be treated with appropriate insecticidal sprays. Hosing leaves may bring temporary relief but if infestations are bad, cut the plants back to ground level. Plants affected by root rot, which is caused by bad drainage, should be removed; rotate plants every three years.

Pruning   Prune after flowering to keep plant compact.

HARVESTING

Picking   Pick fresh leaves throughout the growing season as required. Cut whole stems before flowering and hang them up to dry in a cool, shady spot.

Storage   Strip dry leaves from stems and store in airtight jars.

Freezing   Put leaves in a freezer bag; can be frozen for up to 6 months.

USES

Culinary   Oregano is widely used as a flavouring, especially in Mediterranean-style cooking, in sauces, soups and casseroles, as well as in vinegars and butters.

Gardening   Oregano plants make excellent groundcover.

OREGANO AT A GLANCE

Oregano is a widely grown perennial herb, popular as a flavouring in Mediterranean-style cooking. Hardy to minus 15°C.

JAN	/		
FEB	/		*Parts used*
MAR	plant		Leaves
APR	plant		
MAY	plant	harvest	*Uses*
JUN	plant	harvest	Culinary
JULY	plant	harvest	Gardening
AUG	plant	harvest	
SEPT		harvest	
OCT	/		
NOV	/		
DEC	/		

PARSLEY
Petroselinum

NO NEED TO DESPAIR *when parsley flowers as the flowers are edible too. This Italian parsley can also be used in flower arrangements.*

HERE GROWING *with lettuces, sage and nasturtiums, curly parsley makes a very attractive addition to any bed of herbs and vegetables.*

CURLY PARSLEY *is the prettiest of garnishes and the essential ingredient in a bouquet garni. Here it grows with white alyssum.*

FEATURES

Parsley grows from a strong tap root with erect, 30cm (12in) tall stems bearing divided, feather-like, small leaves which may be flattish or curly depending on variety. Tiny, yellowish-green flower clusters are borne on tall stalks in summer, and produce small, brown, oval and ribbed seeds. Common varieties of this biennial or short-lived perennial plant include curly parsley, *P. crispum*, plain-leaved or Italian parsley, *P. crispum* var. *neapolitanum*, and Hamburg or turnip-rooted parsley, *P. crispum* var. *tuberosum*.

CONDITIONS

Aspect   Grow in full sun or light shade.
Site   Parsley plants like a rich, deep, well-drained soil.

GROWING METHOD

Sowing and planting   Sow seed under cover in spring in pots or plug trays rather than seed trays as parsley dislikes being transplanted. The seed can be difficult to germinate so help to create optimum conditions by soaking the seeds in warm water for 24 hours and then pouring boiling water over the soil to raise the temperature. Plant the young seedlings out, 15cm (6in) apart, after they have grown several true leaves. If parsley is grown in containers, the pots should be at least 20cm (8in) deep, and the longer tap root of Hamburg parsley will require a pot that is even deeper. Once parsley plants are established in the garden, the mature plants can be left to self-sow when they go to seed during the summer months in their second year of growth.

Feeding   Keep the soil moist and do not let it dry out in dry weather. Occasional feeds of a nitrogen-rich liquid fertiliser will promote more leaf growth.

Problems   Carrot fly and root aphids can be particular problems. Destroy affected plants. Slugs also love young plants.

Pruning   Parsley can be kept productive by frequent pruning and by nipping out the flower stalks whenever they appear.

ITS FINE TEXTURE AND RICH GREEN COLOUR makes parsley an ideal edging plant. Here it is used to set off the varied tones and textures of a formal vegetable garden, but it would look equally fine as a foil for brightly coloured flowers.

HARVESTING

Picking	New growth comes from the centre of the stem, and so always pick parsley from the outside of the plant. Pick this vitamin-rich, nutritious herb as needed. Dig up young roots of Hamburg parsley in autumn.
Storage	Broad-leaved Italian parsley, with its stronger taste, gives a better result when dried than the other varieties.
Freezing	Curly parsley freezes well. Put sprigs in freezer bags and freeze for up to 6 months.

USES

Culinary	Parsley is used in salads, as a garnish and in cooking. Hamburg parsley is used as a root vegetable.
Cosmetic	An infusion can be used as a hair rinse. Chew raw parsley to promote a healthy skin.
Medicinal	Parsley is very nutritious and it is a strong diuretic. Fresh parsley is a breath freshener, and is recommended for taking away the smell of garlic on the breath. It has been used in poultices and to make an antiseptic dressing for wounds and bites. *Caution:* Do not use medicinally during pregnancy.
Gardening	Parsley makes an attractive edging plant.

PARSLEY AT A GLANCE

Parsley, with its tasty green leaves, is one of the best known of all the culinary herbs. Frost hardy to minus 15°C or below.

JAN	/		*Parts used*	
FEB	/		Leaves	
MAR	plant		Flowers	
APR	plant	harvest	Roots	
MAY	plant	harvest		
JUN	plant	harvest	*Uses*	
JULY		harvest	Culinary	
AUG		harvest	Medicinal	
SEPT		harvest	Cosmetic	
OCT	/		Gardening	
NOV	/			
DEC	/			

PINKS
Dianthus

FEATURES

Popular garden plants, pinks are very pretty, short-lived, hardy perennials. A wide range of species and varieties is available, which vary in height from about 15cm (6in) to 60cm (24in.) or more. One of those with the longest herbal tradition is *Dianthus caryophyllus*, the clove carnation. The rich, sweet, clove scent of the flowers has made it popular in perfumery for more than 2000 years. Generally pinks have narrow, grey-green, lance-shaped leaves. The flowers appear in spring or summer, in shades of pink or white, and are usually highly fragrant. Plants can become straggly after a few years, and are best discarded and replaced with young plants that have been grown from cuttings.

CONDITIONS

Aspect Pinks prefer a sunny, sheltered site.
Site Grow them in a very well-drained soil that is not too rich, and preferably alkaline.

GROWING METHOD

Sowing and Planting Pinks can be grown from seed, but the resulting plants can be very variable. Sow the seed under glass in trays of gritty seed compost in spring or autumn. Take care not to overwater and be sure to ventilate well. Plant out in spring, after hardening off, at about 30cm (1ft) apart. Named forms can be propagated by cuttings, division or layering. Take cuttings in late summer. Plants can also be layered at this time of year. The plants can also be dug up after they have finished flowering, and any rooted stems can be severed and replanted.

Feeding Pinks tolerate relatively dry conditions. Be careful not to overwater. Pinks need little

DIVINE FLOWERS: The name Dianthus comes from the words 'dios', meaning divine, and 'anthos', meaning flower.

feeding. A light dressing of a balanced general fertiliser may be given in early spring. Do not mulch as this can cause the stems to rot.

Problems The main pest is red spider mite. Also virus, leaf spots and leaf-attacking insects may cause problems.

Pruning Remove dead flowerheads to prolong flowering.

HARVESTING

Picking Pick flowers when newly open. If the petals are to be used in cooking, remove the white heel from each of the petals as this has a very bitter flavour.

Storage Dry on racks in a cool, airy place. Petals can also be crystallised.

Freezing Not suitable for freezing.

USES

Culinary Fresh petals can be used in salads, and also puddings and savoury dishes. They can also be used to flavour oils, vinegar, syrup or white wine. Crystallised petals can be used to decorate cakes and puddings.

Medicinal The petals can be used to make a tonic cordial, or can be infused in white wine to make a nerve tonic.

Craft Dried petals can be used to add colour and scent to pot-pourri mixes, and used to make scented sachets etc.

Cosmetic Fresh petals can be used to scent a variety of cosmetic products.

Gardening Pinks are amongst the most decorative of all the garden herbs.

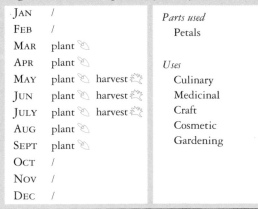

PINKS AT A GLANCE

Attractive perennials with highly fragrant flowers, which have a long tradition of use in perfumery. Hardy to minus 15°C.

JAN	/		
FEB	/		
MAR	plant		
APR	plant		
MAY	plant	harvest	
JUN	plant	harvest	
JULY	plant	harvest	
AUG	plant		
SEPT	plant		
OCT	/		
NOV	/		
DEC	/		

Parts used
Petals

Uses
Culinary
Medicinal
Craft
Cosmetic
Gardening

POT MARIGOLD
Calendula officinalis

FEATURES

A bushy hardy annual with light green leaves and brightly coloured flowers in shades of orange from spring to autumn. The traditional cottage garden pot marigolds have single, bright orange flowers, but many more decorative double and semi-double varieties are readily available. However, if these are allowed to self-seed, which they will do freely, the single form will eventually come to dominate again.

CONDITIONS

Aspect   Pot marigolds grow best in full sun or light shade. They can become leggy if grown in deeper shade.

Site   Pot marigolds are very tolerant plants, growing in most soils that do not get waterlogged, but they do best in well-drained, not too rich soils.

GROWING METHOD

Sowing and planting   Propagate from seed sown in spring or autumn.
Plant out 30–45cm (12–18in) apart. Pot marigolds will self-sow freely.

Feeding   Do not allow the soil to become waterlogged. No special feeding required.

Problems   Slugs may eat the young leaves. Blackfly may be a problem late in the season. Cut out infested areas and spray with horticultural soap. Mildew may also be a problem, but generally this does not occur until flowering is over. Remove and burn affected parts to prevent it from spreading.

Pruning   No special requirements. Pinch out growing tips to prevent the plant becoming leggy. Deadhead regularly to encourage continuous flowering.

POT MARIGOLD AT A GLANCE

A popular annual herb with brightly coloured flowers that have a wide range of herbal uses. Hardy to minus 15°C or below.

JAN	/		*Parts used*
FEB	/		Flowers
MAR	plant		Leaves
APR	plant		
MAY	plant	harvest	
JUN		harvest	*Uses*
JULY		harvest	Culinary
AUG		harvest	Medicinal
SEPT	plant		Cosmetic
OCT	/		Craft
NOV	/		Gardening
DEC	/		

IN THE AMERICAN CIVIL WAR doctors on the battlefield used marigold flowers to treat the soldiers' wounds.

HARVESTING

Picking   Pick the flowers just as they open for use fresh or dry. Pick leaves when they are young for fresh use.

Storage   Dry pot marigold flowers slowly at low temperatures, on a non-metal rack in a cool airy place.

Freezing   The petals can be frozen in ice cubes and used as required to decorate drinks.

USES

Culinary   Petals can be used fresh in salads, butters and cheeses, and also in cooked dishes including omelettes, soups, etc. They can also be used to add colour to rice dishes. Young leaves can also be added to salads.

Medicinal   Pot marigold flowers have antiseptic, anti-fungal and anti-bacterial properties and have traditionally been used medicinally for a wide range of conditions, including the treatment of wounds, burns, stings and bites, chilblains and varicose veins. An infusion was also used as an eyewash. The sap from the stem is said to remove warts.

Cosmetic   Pot marigold can be used to make a range of cosmetic preparations. For example, infused flowers can be used to make skin and hair care preparations. Used in a skin lotion, they are said to help clear up spots.

Craft   The dried petals can be used to add colour to pot-pourri. The fresh petals produce a yellow dye.

Gardening   A traditional and popular cottage garden flower. Being sensitive to temperature, they give an indication of the weather. Open flowers are said to forecast a fine day.

PURSLANE
Portulaca oleracea

FEATURES

This spreading, succulent annual is very adaptable, growing as a weed in many parts of the world. Purslane forms a mat-like growth, which makes it a useful groundcover in areas where it will not spread unduly. It has bright, light green, spoon-shaped leaves on trailing, fleshy stems that are reddish in colour. The small, bright yellow flowers are produced at stem junctions during the summer months. They will open only when the plants are in sunlight. A golden-leaved form *P.o.* 'Sativa' is available.

CONDITIONS

Aspect Full sun is preferable but plants will tolerate shade for part of the day.

Site Purslane is not fussy about soil so long as it drains freely, but plants will produce succulent leaves more quickly if grown in fertile, sandy soil containing some well-rotted organic matter.

GROWING METHOD

Sowing and planting Sow the seeds directly where they are to grow in late spring or summer, with 30cm (12in) between the rows, and thin to 10–15cm (4–6in) between plants. Purslane can also be started from cuttings that are taken any time from mid-spring onwards. Make the cuttings about 5cm (2in) long, strip off the lower leaves and insert the cuttings into small containers of very sandy potting mix or seed compost. Keep the containers warm and moist, and put them in a bright but not sunny spot until the roots have formed. The plants can then be planted out in the garden in their permanent positions.

Feeding Having water-storing leaves and stems, purslane is well able to cope with dryness, but for the best quality leaves keep the soil evenly

PICK ONLY THE TENDEREST YOUNG LEAVES, preferably before plants flower. Old leaves are apt to be tough and tasteless.

moist during spring and summer. Feeding will not be necessary if purslane is grown in fertile soil. Elsewhere, water the plants once a month with a high nitrogen, soluble fertiliser.

Problems No pest or disease problems. Remove flowers to minimise unwanted spread by seed.

HARVESTING

Picking Let the plants grow until they are about 10cm (4in) across and then pick the stems and leaves as they are needed. The plants will regrow quickly.

Storage Cut purslane stems may be stored in the refrigerator for a few days.

Freezing Not suitable for freezing.

USES

Culinary Leaves and stems contain large amounts of iron and vitamin C and have a fresh, acid taste. They may be eaten raw in salads, or they can be lightly stir-fried or steamed as a vegetable, or pickled in vinegar.

Medicinal A cooling herb, used to reduce fevers and clear toxins. Effective against many bacterial infections.

PURSLANE AT A GLANCE

A spreading, succulent annual, grown for stems and leaves which are used as a vegetable. Hardy to minus 5°C at best.

JAN	/	
FEB	/	
MAR	/	
APR	plant 🌱	
MAY	plant 🌱	
JUN	plant 🌱	harvest 🍂
JULY		harvest 🍂
AUG		harvest 🍂
SEPT		harvest 🍂
OCT	/	
NOV	/	
DEC	/	

Parts used
Leaves
Stems

Uses
Culinary
Medicinal

ROSA GALLICA

Rosa gallica var. *officinalis*

FEATURES

A prickly shrub that can reach a height of 1.2m (4ft), the apothecary's rose, *Rosa gallica*, is a dense bush that spreads by suckers, often forming impenetrable thickets. The fragrant, semi-double, deep pink-red flowers appear in summer, followed in autumn by dull red hips. Leaves are elliptical in shape and leathery.

CONDITIONS

Aspect
From south-east Europe and western Asia, apothecary's rose is best grown in full sun. An open site with good air movement helps reduce fungal diseases.

Site
Grows in a wide range of soil types but drainage must be good, especially in areas of high summer rainfall. Deep, friable clay-loam with plenty of well-rotted organic matter is best.

GROWING METHOD

Sowing and planting
Can be grown from seed collected from ripe hips in autumn but sown in spring, or from suckers detached from the parent plant in late winter. Each sucker must have its own roots; replant at once. Take hardwood cuttings about 20cm (8in) long in late autumn; insert them into potting compost or vacant garden beds and keep moist. Rooted cuttings can be potted up or planted into the garden a year later.

Feeding
Established plants can survive on rain alone in areas of regular rainfall but the plant will look and flower better if given an occasional deep soaking during dry spells in summer. Give a balanced general rose fertiliser in spring. Mulch in spring with well-rotted organic matter to improve the soil, feed the plant and conserve moisture.

Problems
Suffers from the usual rose problems: aphids, caterpillars, scale insects and fungus diseases,

THE 'RED ROSES' in old recipes always meant the apothecary's rose, but you can substitute any sweetly scented red rose from your garden.

especially in humid conditions. Combined insecticide/fungicide, usually sold as 'rose spray', controls aphids, caterpillars and fungus diseases, and may also include a foliar feed.

Pruning
Does not need annual pruning and can be left alone for years. To rejuvenate an old bush, cut stems to the ground in winter.

HARVESTING

Picking
Hips are harvested in autumn when fully ripe; flowers can be picked for immediate use as they appear.

Storage
Both hips and flowers may be stored for a few days in sealed containers in the refrigerator. The petals can be dried for use in pot-pourris, herbal sachets, etc.

Freezing
Rose hips and flowers are best used fresh.

USES

Culinary
Rosehips are made into jellies, syrups and liqueurs (all have a very high proportion of vitamin C). Petals are used to flavour vinegar or are crystallised and eaten as a sweet.

Medicinal
Infusions made from the hips and/or petals are said to be good for headaches and a range of other common complaints such as diarrhoea, fever, mouth ulcers and toothache.

Craft
Hips and petals are used in crafts. Dried petals are added to pot-pourris. Attar of roses, an essence extracted from the flowers, is a perfuming agent.

Cosmetic
Petals can be used to perfume creams, etc.

Gardening
This makes a good large-scale groundcover, barrier planting or hedge.

ROSA GALLICA AT A GLANCE

The apothecary's rose is a prickly shrub, grown for its vivid, highly perfumed flowers and its hips. Hardy to minus 15°C or below.

JAN	/		
FEB	plant	*Parts used*	
MAR	plant	Flowers	
APR	/	Hips	
MAY	/		
JUN		harvest	
JULY		harvest	*Uses*
AUG	/		Culinary
SEPT		harvest	Medicinal
OCT	plant / harvest		Craft
NOV	plant		Cosmetic
DEC	/		Gardening

ROSEMARY
Rosmarinus officinalis

THIS STANDARD ROSEMARY grows in a pot with Mexican daisies providing a dash of colour around its base.

TRADITIONALLY a bringer of good fortune, rosemary is often grown by a path or steps, where its fragrance can also be enjoyed as you pass.

FEATURES

A perennial, evergreen, woody shrub, rosemary has thin, needle-like leaves, which are glossy green above and are whitish to grey-green and hairy below. They have a fragrance reminiscent of pine needles. In spring, small-lobed flowers appear among the leaves. They are pale blue to pinkish or white, depending on the variety. There are several varieties of rosemary, ranging in habit from the upright (*R. officinalis*) to the dwarf (*R. officinalis* 'Nana') and the prostrate (*R. officinalis* 'Prostratus'). Among the many very popular varieties are 'Miss Jessop's Upright' (which is very good for hedges) and pink rosemary (*R. officinalis* 'Roseus'). Rosemary bushes can be between 50cm (20in) and 2m (6ft 6in) in height, depending on variety. This is a good herb to grow in containers, and it also grows well in seaside positions where not much else will grow, as it will withstand salt.

CONDITIONS

Aspect Rosemary likes a sunny, sheltered and reasonably dry position. Although hardy in most areas, protection is advised in severe weather and in colder areas, particularly for young plants.

Site Rosemary needs to be grown in a well-drained soil in order to lessen the risk of root rot, and the plant is more fragrant when it is grown in alkaline soils.

GROWING METHOD

Sowing and planting Propagate mainly from cuttings and layering. Seeds are not often used because they have long germination times and tend not to come true to type. Take 10cm (4in) long cuttings in late spring or early autumn, trim off the upper and lower leaves and place the cuttings in small pots containing a moist mixture of two-thirds coarse sand and one-third compost. Cover with a plastic dome and set aside in a semi-shaded position until roots and new leaves form. Or layer by scarifying the underside of a lower branch and firmly securing it to the soil with a wire peg. Cover with sand and keep moist until roots form. Cut off and replant.

Feeding Prefers soil to be on the drier side; give average garden watering. Mulch in spring and also give an application of a balanced general fertiliser at this time.

Problems No particular problems.

Pruning Prune if compact bushes are desired. Trim after flowering to prevent plants becoming straggly. Do not cut back in autumn or when there is a danger of frosts as the plants could be damaged.

HARVESTING

Picking Fresh leaves or sprigs 5–10cm (2–4in) long can be picked as required. Pick flowers in spring.

Storage Dry sprigs in a cool, dry place, strip leaves from the stems and store in airtight jars.

Freezing Store sprigs in plastic bags and freeze for up to 6 months. To use, crumble before they thaw.

ROSEMARY BUSHES will take hard pruning but don't cut into leafless wood, which will not sprout. That's what has happened here.

ROSEMARY FLOWERS have a subtle scent, sweeter than the leaves. They are usually blue, but can be pink or white.

USES

Culinary	Fresh, dried or frozen leaves are used in cooking, marinades and salad dressings. Fresh leaves are used in vinegars, oils, teas and butters. Fresh flowers are good in salads or as decorations for puddings and desserts.
Medicinal	Rosemary has many uses, including treatment for headaches, digestive problems and poor circulation. It has anti-bacterial and anti-fungal properties, and can also be used as an insect repellant. *Caution:* do not use in large doses.
Craft	It is used in pot-pourris and herb wreaths.
Cosmetic	Rosemary hair rinses help control greasy hair.

ROSEMARY AT A GLANCE

Evergreen shrub with fragrant leaves and flowers, much used in cooking and crafts. Hardiness varies: minus 5 to minus 15°C.

JAN		harvest	*Parts used*
FEB		harvest	Leaves
MAR	plant	harvest	Flowers
APR	plant	harvest	
MAY	plant	harvest	*Uses*
JUN	plant	harvest	Culinary
JULY	plant	harvest	Medicinal
AUG	plant	harvest	Craft
SEPT		harvest	Cosmetic
OCT		harvest	Gardening
NOV		harvest	
DEC		harvest	

'SEVEN SEAS' has the richest blue flowers of any rosemary cultivar. Its growth is upright, but less dense and compact than most rosemaries.

RUE

Ruta graveolens

FEATURES

Rue, (*Ruta graveolens*) is a handsome, evergreen, shrubby perennial with many stems rising from a woody base. It can grow to about 60cm (24in) tall with a similar spread. Leaves are strongly aromatic, blue-green and finely divided, making an attractive background for the small, spicily fragrant, yellowish flowers which appear in summer. Two attractive varieties that are readily available are 'Jackman's Blue', a compact plant with steely-blue foliage, and 'Variegata', which has leaves flecked with creamy white. *Caution:* the plant's sap can severely irritate sensitive skins. Wear gloves whenever the plant is handled and do not let it touch hands, face or body.

CONDITIONS

Aspect Rue prefers a sunny position but will tolerate some light shade. It is reasonably hardy, only requiring protection in extreme conditions.

Site Deep, well-drained but rather poor, sandy or gravelly soil suits rue. In its native range it grows in dry, rocky places on limestone soils. Over-rich soils lead to lax, rampant growth and loss of compactness.

GROWING METHOD

Sowing and planting Sow seeds in spring in trays of seed compost. Keep moist and place in bright, dappled shade. Gradually expose young plants to greater amounts of sun before planting into the final position. Alternatively, new plants can be grown from cuttings taken in summer. Select growth that has matured but is not yet woody and place 10cm (4in) cuttings into pots of very sandy potting mix. Keep the compost moist and place pots in bright shade until roots have formed. Where stems of

MEDIEVAL MONKS believed rue encouraged chastity and grew it in their gardens, calling it 'herb of grace'. They also used it to kill fleas.

mature plants touch the ground, they will often form roots. These rooted 'layers' can be detached from the parent plant and relocated.

Feeding Water in summer only in dry areas and only if the plant looks as if it needs water. No feeding is needed.

Problems Usually no pest and disease problems but rue can sometimes suffer from whitefly and sooty mould. Treat with horticultural soap at the first sign.

Pruning Untidy plants may be pruned hard in early spring. Using sharp secateurs, cut back to a main framework of branches. New growth will restore the plant's rounded, bushy habit. Keep plants more compact by a light, all-over shearing in mid-spring.

HARVESTING

Picking Rue has toxic properties and must be used with extreme caution. Leaves may be picked at any time to make an insecticidal infusion.

Storage Leafy stems may be bunched and dried in a dark, airy place for later use.

Freezing Not suitable for freezing.

USES

Culinary Leaves can be eaten but are extremely bitter.

Medicinal Although an ancient medical herb, rue should not be used without professional supervision.

Gardening A decorative plant that infuses the garden with its herbal aroma, especially on hot days. It is a good companion for other Mediterranean plants such as lavender and echium. An insect repellent for use on ornamental or productive plants can be made from the leaves.

RUE AT A GLANCE

A handsome, decorative, aromatic evergreen shrubby perennial with insect repellent properties. Hardy to about minus 15°C.

JAN		harvest 🌿	*Parts used*
FEB		harvest 🌿	Leaves
MAR	plant 🖐	harvest 🌿	
APR	plant 🖐	harvest 🌿	
MAY	plant 🖐	harvest 🌿	*Uses*
JUN	plant 🖐	harvest 🌿	(Culinary)
JULY	plant 🖐	harvest 🌿	(Medicinal)
AUG		harvest 🌿	Gardening
SEPT		harvest 🌿	
OCT		harvest 🌿	
NOV		harvest 🌿	
DEC		harvest 🌿	

SAGE
Salvia

PURPLE SAGE grows here in this wonderfully exuberant herb and vegetable garden, contributing to the subtle harmony of colours. It has cotton lavender growing on its left and a fancy-leaved lettuce on its right.

FEATURES

Sage is an evergreen sub-shrub growing to about 75cm (30in). The long, oval, grey-green leaves, velvety in texture, have a slightly bitter, camphor-like taste, while the flowers, borne on spikes in spring, are coloured from pink to red, purple, blue or white, depending on variety. There are many varieties of this beautiful herb. The most common hardy edible types are common or garden sage (*S. officinalis*), purple sage (*S. o.* 'Purpurascens'), and golden or variegated sage (*S. officinalis* 'Icterina'); and the more tender tricolour sage (*S. o.* 'Tricolor') and pineapple sage (*S. elegans*, syn. *S. rutilans*) are also popular. Sage needs to be replaced every four years or so as the plant becomes woody. Many ornamental sages are also grown in gardens.

CONDITIONS

Aspect   Most varieties prefer a sunny, sheltered, well-drained position.

Site   Garden beds in which sage is to be grown should have a rich, non-clayish soil. Add lime to acid soils, followed by plenty of organic matter. Good drainage is absolutely essential for sage plants, and so you may find it

necessary to raise the beds to at least 20cm (8in) above the surrounding level.

GROWING METHOD

Sowing and planting   Common sage can be grown from seed. Germination takes 2–3 weeks. Plant out when

SAGE AT A GLANCE

Evergreen shrub with silver-grey leaves used in the kitchen for stuffing, herb teas, etc. Hardiness varies: minus 5 to minus 15°C.

JAN	/		*Parts used*
FEB	/		Leaves
MAR	plant 🖐	harvest 🌿	Flowers
APR	plant 🖐	harvest 🌿	
MAY	plant 🖐	harvest 🌿	*Uses*
JUN	plant 🖐	harvest 🌿	Culinary
JULY		harvest 🌿	Medicinal
AUG		harvest 🌿	Cosmetic
SEPT	plant 🖐	harvest 🌿	Craft
OCT		harvest 🌿	Gardening
NOV	/		
DEC	/		

SALVIA GRAHAMII, very strong in flavour, is a metre-tall shrub from Mexico, usually grown for its long display of bright flowers.

THE PURPLE-BLUE FLOWERS of common sage go very well with its grey leaves. Trim them off when they fade to keep the garden neat.

THE LEAVES of purple sage fade as they mature, but new shoots continue to add touches of colour all summer. Flowers are purple-blue.

all danger of frost is passed, spacing plants 45–60cm (18–24in) apart. Cuttings 10cm (4in) long can be taken in spring or autumn. Remove the upper and lower leaves and plant the cuttings in small pots containing a mix of two-thirds coarse sand to one-third compost. Water, then cover plants with a plastic bag to create a mini-greenhouse. Plant out when the cutting has developed roots and new leaves. Sage may also be layered; scarify the lower side of a branch and peg it into the soil to take root.

Feeding   Give a deep soaking once a week in dry spells. Apply a balanced general fertiliser in spring.

Problems   Spider mites can be a problem and will need to be sprayed with an insecticide. If the plant suddenly flops over for no apparent reason this is probably due to bacterial wilt affecting the vascular system. Remove affected plants. Root rot can be avoided by providing good drainage.

Pruning   Prune in spring to keep a compact, bushy shape. Cut off flowerheads as the flowers fade to stop plants from setting seed.

HARVESTING

Picking   Leaves or flowers can be picked at any time as required. For drying purposes, harvest leaves before flowering begins.

Storage   Dry leaves on racks in a cool, airy place and then store them in airtight jars.

Freezing   Leaves can be chopped, packed in freezer bags and then frozen for up to 6 months.

USES

Culinary   Fresh or dried leaves are used extensively as a flavouring in stuffings, marinades and cooking. The individual fruity flavour of pineapple sage complements citrus fruits and the edible flowers look decorative in salads or as a garnish. Sage leaves of many varieties can be used in herbal teas, vinegars and herb butters.

Medicinal   Sage has long been highly regarded for its healing properties. Uses include treating colds, sore throats and mouth ulcers. *Caution:* do not take in large quantities or for extended periods.

Cosmetic   Sage hair rinses, used regularly, will darken grey hair.

Craft   Dried leaves, especially those of purple sage can be added to pot-pourri.

Gardening   It is said that sage can be planted with cabbages to deter cabbage white butterflies.

SALAD BURNET

Sanguisorba minor

THE GREYISH LEAVES OF SALAD BURNET make a pretty, fragrant groundcover. In the old days, doctors used them like cotton wool to absorb the blood from wounds, hence the botanical name Sanguisorba which is derived from the Latin words for 'blood' and 'to suck'.

FEATURES

This small but bushy perennial herb grows in a clump 20–60cm (8–24in) high. The roundish, grey-green, toothed leaves are borne on a central stem which droops down close to the ground. Flower stems appear in summer and produce small round heads of red-green flowers. Salad burnet is an attractive border plant and it can be grown successfully in pots.

CONDITIONS

Aspect Likes an open, sunny position.
Site Most soil types are suitable. Add lime if the soil conditions are acidic. Ensure soil is well drained at all times.

SALAD BURNET AT A GLANCE

Small perennial with 'drumstick' flowers, and grey-green toothed leaves used in salads and drinks. Hardy to minus 15°C or below.

JAN	/		*Parts used*	
FEB	/		Leaves	
MAR	plant			
APR	plant		*Uses*	
MAY	plant	harvest	Culinary	
JUN		harvest	Medicinal	
JULY		harvest	Gardening	
AUG		harvest		
SEPT	plant			
OCT	/			
NOV	/			
DEC	/			

GROWING METHOD

Sowing and planting Salad burnet readily self-sows. Germinate seed in seed trays, cover the seed lightly with perlite and keep damp. When seedlings are 5–10cm (2–4in) tall, plant them out spaced 30–40cm (12–16in) apart. Propagation by division during autumn or spring is also possible.

Feeding Water plants thoroughly in hot weather, before signs of wilting. Apply a balanced general fertiliser once each year in early spring and water in well.

Problems Burnet suffers from root rot if the soil is not well drained. If conditions are too damp in winter crown rot will develop and the plants will turn yellow and die.

Pruning Removal of flowers will stimulate leaf growth.

HARVESTING

Picking Pick the leaves when young and tender.
Storage Cannot be successfully stored.
Freezing Cannot be frozen.

USES

Culinary Use burnet only when fresh. Leaves have a cucumber scent and flavour and are much prized in salads, with fresh vegetables or as a garnish. They can also be chopped and included in cooked soups or sauces, and in herb butter and vinegar. Freshly picked sprigs look effective as a garnish in summer drinks.

Medicinal An infusion was used to treat diarrhoea, and staunch wounds.

Gardening As a companion plant, burnet does very well if grown close by beds of thyme and mint.

SALAD ROCKET

Eruca vesicaria subspecies *sativa*

FEATURES

Rocket is an annual with long, deeply lobed, dark green leaves, often tinted red, and simple, cross-shaped, creamy-white flowers. Leaves have a pleasant, peppery, nutty flavour and are produced in a dense rosette at the base of the plant, from which rise the branching stems. The stems, which may reach 60–90cm (2–3ft), bear flowers, followed by plump seedheads which shatter when dry, each dispersing hundreds of seeds. Rocket grows very fast and will be ready to pick within 6–8 weeks of sowing. Several crops may be raised during spring and summer.

CONDITIONS

Aspect   During spring grows best in full sun or light shade, but in summer a partly shaded spot helps slow the plant's rush to seed and thus lengthens its useful life.

Site   Grow in fertile, well-drained soil enriched with well-rotted manure or compost. Rocket will grow in poor soils, too, but its leaves will be tough and more bitter.

GROWING METHOD

Sowing and planting   It is best to sow the seeds where they are to grow from early spring to mid summer, making earliest sowings under cloches. Space rows 12cm (5in) apart and thin to 30cm (12in) between plants. They can be sown indoors in trays of seed compost on a sunny window. Plant out when danger of frost has passed. As rocket grows fast and young leaves are most palatable, new sowings should be made about every four weeks. When the latest batch of seedlings is big enough to pick from, pull out the previous batch. You can continue sowing rocket until about mid autumn.

ROCKET was loved by the Romans and remains a favourite salad herb in Italy. It is a native of the Mediterranean.

Feeding   For fastest growth and sweetest, best tasting leaves, keep plants well watered. Plants enjoy consistent moisture but not wetness around the roots, so make sure the soil drains well. Rake in a ration of a balanced general fertiliser at sowing time and then water the plants over every two weeks or so with a soluble, high nitrogen fertiliser.

Problems   Snails and slugs may damage leaves of young plants in early spring and autumn. Hand pick them at night by torchlight. Rocket can quickly become an invasive weed so it is important to prevent flowering except to provide seeds for resowing. On most plants, snap off flower stems as they rise or, better still, replace flowering plants with new, young plants.

HARVESTING

Picking   Start picking young leaves about six weeks after seedlings have emerged, sooner in summer when growth is faster. Seeds are harvested when the pods have plumped out and are beginning to look dry.

Storage   Seeds may be stored in airtight jars but leaves must be used fresh.

Freezing   Not suitable for freezing.

USES

Culinary   Young leaves give green salads an appealing piquancy or add them late to stir frys. Ripe seed pods are also edible. Rocket has recently become fashionable in smart restaurants.

Medicinal   Rocket is said to be a stimulant and good for warding off colds. It was once used to make cough syrup.

SALAD ROCKET AT A GLANCE

An annual herb, grown for its peppery, nutty flavoured leaves, used in salads and stir fries. Hardy to minus 15°C or below.

Month	Activity		Parts used
JAN	/		
FEB	/		Leaves
MAR	plant		Seeds
APR	plant	harvest	Seed pods
MAY	plant	harvest	
JUN	plant	harvest	
JULY	plant	harvest	*Uses*
AUG	plant	harvest	Culinary
SEPT	plant	harvest	Medicinal
OCT		harvest	
NOV	/		
DEC	/		

SANTOLINA
Santolina chamaecyparissus

FEATURES

Grey, rounded and cushiony, santolina, or cotton lavender, is a low, ground-covering, evergreen sub-shrub that usually grows about 45–60cm (18–24in) tall. When crushed, the toothed leaves give off a strong aroma reminiscent of lavender but with a delightful difference. In summer, yellow button flowers appear on leafless stems and make a striking contrast to the soft grey leaves. It is an ideal plant for hedging and edging.

CONDITIONS

Aspect Originally from the Mediterranean region, cotton lavender prefers full sun.

Site Good drainage is essential but, given that, cotton lavender grows well in poor, rather dry soils. If conditions are too rich it loses its dense, compact appearance and becomes straggly and lax. This plant will tolerate alkaline soils.

GROWING METHOD

Sowing and planting In late spring, take 7.5cm (3in) long cuttings of stems that have lost their sappy freshness but have not yet become woody. Insert the cuttings into small containers of sandy potting compost, keep it moist and the container shaded until roots develop after 4–6 weeks. Harden off the cuttings by moving the container into full sun in stages so as not to burn the leaves that have become used to shade. When fully hardened off, plant out the new plants about 45–60cm (18–24in) apart.

Feeding Once established, cotton lavender is tolerant of dry weather. No fertilising is needed.

Problems High summer rainfall and humidity can cause the plant to rot. If grown in rich soil it may suffer from aphids.

THE SHARP, YELLOW FLOWERS of cotton lavender can upset a grey and silver scheme. If they upset you, trim them in spring.

Pruning Shear the plant all over once or twice during the summer months and once again more heavily in autumn. This will keep the plant neat and very bushy. Make one of the cuts after flowering to keep the compact shape and prevent the bush opening up and becoming straggly.

HARVESTING

Picking Sprigs of leaves may be picked at any time as they are required.

Storage Tie sprigs of the leaves together and hang them upside down in a dark, airy place to dry. Then you can store the dried sprigs in an airtight container.

Freezing Not suitable for freezing.

USES

Craft Dried leaves can be used in pot-pourris and herbal sachets. It can be used to deter moths.

Gardening Cotton lavender is mostly used today as an edging plant along paths or drives or to border herb or vegetable gardens or other formal plantings. It can also be used as an unusual large-scale groundcover, especially if used on dry, sunny banks.

SANTOLINA AT A GLANCE

Silvery leaved, rounded sub-shrub. The leaves have a strong aroma and are used in pot-pourris etc. Hardy to minus 10°C.

JAN		harvest	*Parts used*	
FEB		harvest	Leaves	
MAR		harvest	Sprigs	
APR		harvest		
MAY	plant	harvest	*Uses*	
JUN	plant	harvest	Craft	
JULY		harvest	Garden	
AUG		harvest		
SEPT	plant	harvest		
OCT		harvest		
NOV		harvest		
DEC		harvest		

SAVORY
Satureja

BOTH SAVORIES, winter and summer, are alike in their four-petalled, white flowers. This is the perennial winter savory.

SUMMER SAVORY, being an annual, has to be sown afresh each spring. Many cooks consider it superior in flavour to winter savory.

FEATURES

Summer savory (*S. hortensis*) is an annual plant growing to about 30cm (1ft) and with small, narrow, greyish leaves that turn slightly purple during summer and early autumn. The leaves are attached directly to a pinkish stem, and small white flowers appear on the plant in summer. The winter savories, both the upright (*S. montana*) and the prostrate (*S. montana* 'Repens') varieties, are perennial forms and have low-growing (they may reach 30cm (1ft)) or sprawling habits. Glossy, dark green, lanceolate leaves grow from woody stems in summer and white to lilac flowers are grouped in terminal spikes.

CONDITIONS

Aspect   Both varieties of savory prefer to be grown in full sun. They do not like very cold, wet conditions, and winter savory may require some winter protection.

Site   Savories like well-drained, alkaline soils. Use a soil testing kit to see how much lime to add to an acid soil. Summer savory prefers a richer soil and is ideal for container growing; winter savory favours a less rich, rather sandy soil.

GROWING METHOD

Sowing and planting   Sow seeds of summer savory directly into their final garden position in spring, after the weather has warmed up. Lightly cover them with soil and keep the soil around them damp. When the seedlings are established, thin them out to 15cm (6in) apart and give the plants support by mounding soil round the base. Although it can be grown from seed, winter savory is best propagated by cuttings and root division done during either the spring or the autumn. Remove the upper and lower leaves of 8–10cm (4–5in) long cuttings and insert the trimmed stems into a mixture of two-thirds coarse sand and one-third compost. Water the container and cover it with plastic supported on a wire or bamboo frame to make a mini-greenhouse effect. Plant the seedlings out when new leaves appear and a root structure has developed. Pieces of the divided root of the parent plant can be potted up and grown on and later these can be transplanted into the open garden.

Feeding   Water these plants regularly although both summer and winter savories are able to tolerate dry conditions. Mulch winter savory in winter and spring and give a dressing of a balanced general fertiliser in spring.

THE ANCIENT ROMANS considered savory to be the most delightfully fragrant of all herbs: the poet Virgil sang its praises.

WINTER SAVORY is so called because it is available in winter when summer savory dies off – but you can, of course, eat it in summer too.

Problems   Savories are not worried by pests or diseases to any great extent with the exception of root rot, which sometimes can affect the winter varieties. Good drainage is essential for these plants.

Pruning   Winter savory can be pruned in autumn after it has finished flowering, but leaving it unpruned will leave top growth to protect the shoots below. It can be pruned in early spring – this will also provide cuttings from which you can grow new plants.

HARVESTING

Picking   Fresh leaves of both summer and winter varieties can be picked at any time for immediate use or for drying.

Storage   Dry leaves in a cool, airy space and then store them in airtight jars.

Freezing   Pack sprigs in freezer bags and freeze for up to 6 months.

USES

Culinary   Summer savory has a peppery flavour and is called the 'bean herb' as it complements beans and other vegetables. It is also used in herb vinegars and butters. Winter savory is stronger and coarser and has a more piney taste: use it with game meats and terrines. Either summer or winter savory can be used to make savory tea.

Medicinal   Summer savory is said to be good for the digestion, for the treatment of stings, and as a stimulant.

SAVORY AT A GLANCE

Both summer and winter savory have strong flavours and are used in cooking. Hardy to minus 10 to minus 15°C.

JAN		harvest	*Parts used*
FEB		harvest	Leaves
MAR	plant	harvest	
APR	plant	harvest	
MAY	plant	harvest	*Uses*
JUN		harvest	Culinary
JULY		harvest	Medicinal
AUG		harvest	
SEPT	plant	harvest	
OCT		harvest	
NOV		harvest	
DEC		harvest	

SORREL
Rumex scutatus

ELIZABETHAN COOKS used to wrap tough meat in sorrel leaves to tenderise it and add piquant flavour. They also used to make 'green sauce' from chopped young leaves, vinegar and sugar. Try it with roast lamb, as a change from mint sauce.

FEATURES

Rumex scutatus, the French sorrel or buckler leaf sorrel, is a sprawling perennial herb that grows to 30–45cm (12–18in) high. Its heart-shaped leaves are carried on erect stems rather resembling a dock weed. Another member of the family, *R. acetosa*, is known commonly as sour dock. Small green flowers appear on long stalks in summer.

CONDITIONS

Aspect   Prefers sun or semi-shade.
Site   French sorrel needs light, average soil. To promote strong leaf growth, add well-rotted farmyard manures to the soil and mulch well. Tolerates slightly acidic soils.

SORREL AT A GLANCE

French sorrel is a sprawling, weedy looking herb, the leaves of which make a tasty soup. Hardy to minus 15°C or below.

JAN	/	
FEB	/	
MAR	plant 🌱	
APR	plant 🌱	harvest 🌿
MAY	plant 🌱	harvest 🌿
JUN		harvest 🌿
JULY		harvest 🌿
AUG		harvest 🌿
SEPT	plant 🌱	harvest 🌿
OCT		harvest 🌿
NOV	/	
DEC	/	

Parts used
    Leaves

Uses
    Culinary

GROWING METHOD

Sowing and planting   Sow seed directly into the garden during spring. Thin seedlings to 30cm (1ft) apart. Mature plants can be divided in autumn or early spring. To do this, dig up older plants, trim the leaves and stems and replant the divided portions 30–40cm (12–16in) apart.

Feeding   Water regularly. If the soil is left to dry out, the leaves wilt and burn off. Sorrel will benefit from an application of a balanced general fertiliser in spring.

Problems   Snails and slugs attack leaves. Pick them off by hand or set stale beer traps among the beds. (Fill a saucer with beer and set it into the ground with the rim just above soil level.) If leaf miners attack the plant, remove and destroy infected leaves.

Pruning   If you are not growing plants for seed, pinch out the seed-bearing stalks as they appear.

HARVESTING

Picking   Young leaves can be picked throughout the growing season as required. Always pick from the outside of the clump.

Storage   Freshly picked leaves will keep in the refrigerator for a few days if they are stored in a plastic bag.

Freezing   Put leaves in a freezer bag and freeze for up to 6 months.

USES

Culinary   Sorrel used to be cooked and eaten like spinach. Today, because we know it contains a lot of oxalic acid, we use only the small leaves, which have a lemony flavour, in salads or they can be made into a delicious soup.

TANSY
Tanacetum vulgare

FEATURES

Growing up to 1m (39in) tall, tansy is a sprawling perennial with grey-green, finely divided, ferny foliage and heads of yellow, button-like flowers in late summer. The leaves are aromatic and bitter to the taste and the whole plant dies back to ground level over winter. It spreads out by means of creeping roots and can become quite large over time. In smaller areas it will need to be reduced.

CONDITIONS

Aspect Full sun, part-shade or bright, dappled shade are equally suitable for tansy, although full sun produces more compact growth and many more flowers.

Site Any well-drained soil will do. Tansy is an extremely adaptable plant able to grow almost wherever its seed falls.

GROWING METHOD

Sowing and planting Dividing the roots of an established plant is the easiest way to start a new plant quickly. Lift the parent in early spring and cut or pull the creeping roots into sections, each with its own roots. Replant immediately into the permanent site. Tansy may also be started from seed sown in spring or early autumn or from cuttings of semi-ripe stems that are taken in late spring.

Feeding Water sparingly. No feeding is needed.

Problems No particular problems.

Pruning Cut the plants to the ground in autumn. New growth will appear in spring.

HARVESTING

Picking Pick leafy stems any time during the warmer

THE AROMA OF TANSY is said to deter flies, and people used to place sprigs of tansy leaves on meat to keep flies off it.

months. If flower stems are to be cut, do this when the flowers are freshly opened.

Storage Both leaves and flowers can be stored dry. To dry either, tie bunches together and hang them in a dim, well-ventilated place or lay them out on drying racks. When the leaves are dry, remove them from their stems and store in airtight jars. Take the dried flowers off the stems and store the flowers in airtight jars.

Freezing Not suitable for freezing.

USES

Medicinal *Caution:* although tansy can be taken for medicinal purposes, it must only be administered by a trained herbal practitioner. Tansy has toxic properties and can be easily taken to excess. It should never be used during pregnancy.

Cosmetic Craft Leaves can be used to make a skin freshener. Include tansy in 'insect repellent' sachets or hang up sprigs to deter flies. Scatter sprigs to deter ants and mice.

Gardening Tansy is a lovely, silvery green plant with very attractive flowers and an aroma that is very pleasant in the garden. Grow it in borders of mixed flowers or in big containers that prevent its unwanted spread.

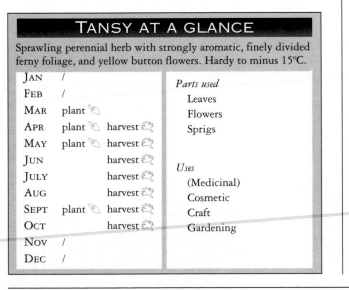

TANSY AT A GLANCE

Sprawling perennial herb with strongly aromatic, finely divided ferny foliage, and yellow button flowers. Hardy to minus 15°C.

Month	Activity		Parts used / Uses
JAN	/		*Parts used*
FEB	/		Leaves
MAR	plant 🖐		Flowers
APR	plant 🖐	harvest ✂	Sprigs
MAY	plant 🖐	harvest ✂	
JUN		harvest ✂	*Uses*
JULY		harvest ✂	(Medicinal)
AUG		harvest ✂	Cosmetic
SEPT	plant 🖐	harvest ✂	Craft
OCT		harvest ✂	Gardening
NOV	/		
DEC	/		

TARRAGON
Artemisia dracunculus

FEATURES

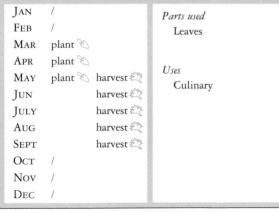

French tarragon (*A. dracunculus*) is a popular culinary herb. It is a half hardy perennial that spreads by rhizomes or underground stems, sending up erect stems to a height of 60–90cm (2–3ft) or more. Leaves are olive green and have an anise flavour. It dies down over winter and regenerates in spring. It must be propagated by division. The tarragon seed offered by some nurseries is Russian tarragon or 'false' tarragon (*A. dracunculus* var. *dracunculoides*). This keeps some of its foliage over winter and is more vigorous, but has a much inferior, more bitter flavour. Tarragon needs to be replanted every few years as plants lose their vigour over time. White or greenish flowers appear in late summer.

CONDITIONS

Aspect   Tarragon does best in a sunny, warm position, but will tolerate partial shade.

Site   Needs well-drained, sandy soils that do not hold moisture for too long, especially over winter when the rhizomes may rot. Dig in some organic matter such as compost and well-rotted farmyard manures.

GROWING METHOD

Sowing and planting   Propagate by root division. Lift the plant during spring, divide it and replant the pieces in pots or in the garden spaced 60cm (2ft) apart. Alternatively, take semi-ripe cuttings in summer.

Feeding   Keep well watered but ease off over winter. Soils should be damp but not soggy. Apply a balanced general fertiliser once in early spring. Mulch French tarragon over winter when it has died down.

Problems   No specific pests but it can suffer from downy

PROLONGED HEAT destroys the flavour of fresh tarragon, and so add it at the end of cooking. Dried tarragon is not affected in this way.

and powdery mildew. Rust may also be a problem. Cut down affected parts and burn them. Root rot may also be a problem.

Pruning   Pick out flower stems to promote leaf growth. Cut back to ground level in autumn.

HARVESTING

Picking   Pick leaves during summer but take care not to bruise them.

Storage   Leaves can be dried although much of the flavour and some of the colour will be lost in the process. Place them on racks or hang stems in bunches in a warm, dry place, and then store them in airtight jars. Leaves can be preserved in vinegar.

Freezing   Put leaves in freezer bags and freeze for up to 6 months.

USES

Culinary   Tarragon is one of the classic French *fines herbes* used to enhance the flavours of sundry foods from fish, meat and dairy foods to herbed vinegars, butters, creamy sauces, vegetables and soups. The leaves of Russian tarragon lack the aromatic oils of the French variety, and have an inferior flavour.

TARRAGON AT A GLANCE

French tarragon is a popular culinary herb, with olive green 'anise flavoured' leaves. Hardy to minus 5 to minus 10°C.

JAN	/		
FEB	/		
MAR	plant		*Parts used*
APR	plant		Leaves
MAY	plant	harvest	
JUN		harvest	*Uses*
JULY		harvest	Culinary
AUG		harvest	
SEPT		harvest	
OCT	/		
NOV	/		
DEC	/		

Thyme
Thymus

A GARDEN SEAT surrounded by a collection of thymes makes a fragrant resting place. Position the creeping thyme (Thymus serpyllum) in front of the seat as it can be trodden on. Thyme has several cultivars, with white, pink or magenta flowers in spring.

FEATURES

Thyme is one of the most common of garden herbs, and very many varieties are grown. Most thymes are low, creeping plants although some will grow to 25–30cm (10–12in). The shape of the bush and the colour and aroma of the leaves depends on the variety. The leaves are evergreen in shades of green, silver and gold, and small pink or sometimes white flowers are produced in early summer. Not all thymes are used in cooking, the most commonly used varieties including lemon-scented thyme (*T.* x *citriodorus*), caraway thyme (*T. herba-barona*), common garden thyme (*T. vulgaris*), orange thyme (*T. vulgaris* 'Fragrantissimus') and silver posie thyme (*T. vulgaris* 'Silver Posie'). Thyme plants are perennials but usually need replacing every two or three years.

CONDITIONS

Aspect   Prefers full sun or partial shade.
Site   Prefers a light, well-drained, not too rich soil,

ideally neutral or slightly alkaline, and kept on the dry side. Adding compost will help keep the soil friable. The soil should not be too acid, if necessary add lime.

THYME AT A GLANCE

Common garden herbs, thymes are popular not only for cooking but also as garden plants. Hardy to minus 15°C or below.

JAN		harvest	*Parts used*	
FEB		harvest	Leaves	
MAR	plant	harvest	Flowers	
APR	plant	harvest	Sprigs	
MAY	plant	harvest		
JUN	plant	harvest		
JULY		harvest	*Uses*	
AUG		harvest	Culinary	
SEPT	plant	harvest	Medicinal	
OCT		harvest	Craft	
NOV		harvest	Gardening	
DEC		harvest		

GROWING METHOD

Sowing and planting
Thymes can be propagated from seed, but this tends to give inferior plants, and named varieties should be propagated by cuttings, division or layering. If seed is used, sow in spring and take care not to overwater as the seedlings are prone to damping off. Dividing mature plants is the most successful method of propagation. During spring or summer, gently lift the parent plant, cut it into two or three sections, each with good roots, and replant elsewhere in the garden. Cuttings taken in spring or summer and layering are also satisfactory methods of propagation.

Feeding
Do not overwater. Thymes prefer a dryish soil. Water adequately in dry spells. No fertiliser needed.

Problems
Spider mites or aphids can affect this herb. Treat with a recommended insecticidal spray. Root rot will set in if the soil is waterlogged.

Pruning
Prune or clip to prevent woodiness. Trim after flowering to prevent plants becoming straggly.

HARVESTING

Picking
Fresh leaves and flowers can be picked as required or the whole plant can be cut back to within 5cm (2in) of the ground in summer.

Storage
Leaves are dried on the stem by hanging branches in a warm, airy place. Branches are then stripped and stored in airtight jars.

Freezing
Pack in small airtight containers or freezer bags; can be frozen for up to 6 months.

USES

Culinary
Thyme is a classic component of the French bouquet garni. Varieties of thyme add special, individual flavours to many dishes. Both leaves and flowers can be eaten fresh in salads or used as garnishes or as a flavouring to honey, vinegars, stuffings, butters or teas.

Medicinal
Thyme has strong antiseptic properties and is used to treat sore throats and as a mouthwash. *Caution:* avoid during pregnancy.

Craft
Can be added to pot-pourris and herb sachets.

Gardening
Thymes can be grown for their decorative effect as their low, matting habit makes them excellent edging or rockery plants.

'SILVER POSIE', a small, sprawling shrub with white variegated leaves and abundant pale flowers in spring, here offers scent to the passer-by.

ANCIENT GREEKS AND ROMANS considered thyme honey the finest of all, and many modern connoisseurs of honey agree with them.

COMMON THYME, Thymus vulgaris, here sprawls over a carpet of creeping thyme, sometimes called 'Shakespeare's thyme'.

WOOLLY THYME is almost prostrate in habit, its leaves covered in grey fur. The flowers are pale pink but not very abundant.

VALERIAN
Valeriana officinalis

FEATURES

Valerian is a tall, spreading hardy perennial, growing to about 1–1.5m (3–5ft) in height. It is native to Europe and Asia where it is found in grassland and damp meadows, close to streams. It has finely divided mid-green leaves and heads of small white or pale pink flowers that are produced in early summer. Both cats and rats are said to find the smell of valerian attractive, and it is said that the Pied Piper of Hamelin carried the root in order to charm the rats away!

CONDITIONS

Aspect   Valerian will grow in full sun or deep shade, as long as the roots are cool. The plants may need to be staked if they are grown in exposed positions.

Site   Valerian is tolerant of most soils, but prefers moist conditions.

GROWING METHOD

Sowing and planting   Valerian can be propagated by division in spring or autumn, replanting the divisions immediately into well prepared ground. The seed can be sown in spring, directly where it is to grow. But for more reliable results sow the seed under glass in trays of seed compost. Do not cover the seeds as this will delay germination. When the young plants are large enough to handle they should be planted out in the garden approximately 60–90cm (2–3ft) apart. When grown in good conditions, valerian will self-seed.

Feeding   Keep well watered as valerian prefers moist conditions. Mulch lightly in spring and also apply a dressing of a balanced general fertiliser in spring.

IN THE TWO WORLD WARS an infusion made from valerian was used to treat shell-shock and nervous disorders.

Problems   Generally free from pests and diseases.

Pruning   Cut valerian back after flowering to prevent self-seeding. The top growth can be cut down in autumn.

HARVESTING

Picking   Dig up the roots in late autumn, when the plants are in their second or third year of growth.

Storage   To dry, cut the roots into thin slices and dry in an oven at 50–60°C (120–40°F), turning frequently.

Freezing   Not suitable for freezing

USES

Medicinal   Valerian has been used for many centuries for its healing properties. Traditionally, the root has been used for its sedative and anti-spasmodic effects, and for the treatment of a wide range of conditions, including nervous conditions, insomnia, headaches, and exhaustion. *Caution:* Do not take valerian in large doses or for extended periods of time. This herb is best taken only under expert supervision.

Cosmetic   Despite its rather unpleasant aroma, valerian has been used in perfumery.

Gardening   Nowadays, valerian is used more in the garden than for its medicinal properties. Although not the most decorative of herbs, it is useful to add height at the back of the border. It is also said to be a good companion plant, encouraging the growth of nearby vegetables and other plants by stimulating earthworm activity and increasing phosphorus availability.

VALERIAN AT A GLANCE

A tall but undistinguished, strong-smelling herb, with powerful healing properties. Fully hardy to minus 15°C or below.

JAN	/	*Parts used*	
FEB	/	Roots	
MAR	plant 🌱		
APR	plant 🌱	*Uses*	
MAY	plant 🌱	Medicinal	
JUN	/	Cosmetic	
JULY	/	Gardening	
AUG	/		
SEPT	plant 🌱	harvest 🌾	
OCT	plant 🌱	harvest 🌾	
NOV	/		
DEC	/		

VIOLET
Viola odorata

FEATURES

Viola odorata, the sweet violet, is a low-growing perennial just 15cm (6in) tall with a wider spread. The dark green leaves are roundish or kidney-shaped with scalloped edges. Small, very sweetly fragrant flowers appear on short stalks in late winter and early spring. They are usually violet in colour but there are also mauve, blue and white forms. Violets spread rapidly by creeping roots.

CONDITIONS

Aspect
Sun in winter and bright dappled shade in summer are ideal. Flowering is disappointing in too much shade.

Site
Violets tolerate most soils but do best in deep soil rich in well-rotted organic matter, preferably from composted fallen leaves. Soil must drain freely but it must also remain moist between showers or watering.

GROWING METHOD

Sowing and planting
Violets are easily established by division. Lift immediately after flowering and separate the cylindrical runners. Each division should have its own roots but roots usually form later if they are absent. Plant so that the runners are firmly in contact with the soil but not buried. Scatter seed, collected from ripe but unopened seed pods, where it is to grow or, for better germination, onto trays of seed compost. Cover lightly, keep moist and place trays in a bright but shady and cool place. The seedlings can be transplanted when they are big enough to handle.

Feeding
Once established, violets can usually get by on rain where it falls regularly, as long as the soil conditions suit them. If they never go dry for long periods, violets will flourish. Place a mulch of well-rotted manure around plants, but not over the root crown, each spring (this can be hard to do in a densely planted area), or sprinkle a ration of a balanced general fertiliser over the plants in spring. Once or twice during summer, water over the plants with a liquid, organic fertiliser or seaweed-based soil conditioner.

Problems
Lay bait for slugs and snails, which chew holes in the leaves and destroy flowers. Spider mites and aphids can also damage plants by sucking sap. Spider mites should be treated with an insecticide as soon as they are seen. Aphids are easily controlled with low toxicity pyrethrum, garlic or fatty acid sprays. If the plants fail to flower, the cause may be too much or too heavy shade or too much high nitrogen fertiliser.

Pruning
No pruning is necessary, but if flowers fail to form cut all the leaves off in early winter to encourage spring bloom.

VIOLETS are notoriously shy: if your flowers hide, cut plants back in winter so the flowers are displayed against fresh, not-too-tall growth.

HARVESTING

Picking
Pick flowers as they open and leaves as needed.

Storage
Flowers may be crystallised for later use.

Freezing
Not suitable for freezing.

USES

Culinary
Crystallised flowers are used to decorate cakes or eaten as a sweet treat. A sweet syrup and a honey can be made with fresh flowers.

Medicinal
An infusion of the leaves and flowers can be taken to relieve the symptoms of colds, etc.

Craft
Flowers are used in pot-pourris, floral waters.

Gardening
Violets are a very desirable groundcover in partly shaded areas. Posies of cut flowers will fill a room with fragrance.

VIOLET AT A GLANCE

Pretty, low-growing perennial with very sweetly fragrant flowers in late winter. Hardy to minus 15°C or below.

			Parts used
JAN		/	Flowers
FEB		harvest	Leaves
MAR		harvest	
APR	plant	harvest	
MAY	plant	harvest	*Uses*
JUN		harvest	Culinary
JULY		harvest	Medicinal
AUG		harvest	Craft
SEPT	plant		Gardening
OCT		/	
NOV		/	
DEC		/	

WATERCRESS

Nasturtium officinale

DESPITE ITS PEPPERINESS, watercress quenches thirst – at least for a little while – and hunters used to carry sprigs for refreshment.

WATERCRESS needs abundant moisture. One way to give it enough is to grow it as market gardeners do, in an easily flooded trench.

FEATURES

Although European in origin, watercress is now widely used in Asian cuisines. It is a perennial growing from 5–60cm (2–24in) with a spreading habit. Round, dark green leaves composed of several leaflets have a peppery mustard flavour and are carried on fleshy stems. These either float or are submerged in shallow, moving water or root in rich, wet soil. Clusters of small white flowers appear in early summer.

CONDITIONS

Aspect
Prefers a wet, shady place, such as a pond or stream that is protected from both strong winds and winter frosts.

Site
Ideal conditions resemble a clean, running stream. If growing watercress in a container, use very damp, rich soil and top up occasionally with well-rotted garden compost. Do not let the water stagnate: drain off some once a week and top it up with fresh water each time. The water should be alkaline.

GROWING METHOD

Sowing and planting
Grow by root division of a mature plant. Place new pieces into a container with good quality potting mix and then lower it into a waterbed. Seeds can also be sown in spring by placing them on constantly damp compost. Transplant seedlings to a permanent position when they are about 7.5cm (3in) tall.

Feeding
Watercress requires a great deal of water. Apply high nitrogen, soluble plant food every two weeks from spring to late summer.

Problems
Watercress is sometimes subject to fungal diseases, which cause rotting of stems and death of leaves. Remove infected plants.

HARVESTING

Picking
Pick leaves as required.

Storage
Freshly picked leaves will keep in fresh cold water or sealed plastic bags in the refrigerator for a couple of days.

Freezing
Put in a freezer bag; freeze for up to 6 months.

USES

Culinary
Watercress is rich in vitamin C, and is used raw in salads, sandwiches or as a garnish. Chinese tend to cook the herb, making delicious soups.

Medicinal
An infusion of leaves and stems relieves indigestion, rheumatic and bronchial conditions.

Cosmetic
A poultice of crushed leaves cleanses and freshens the skin.

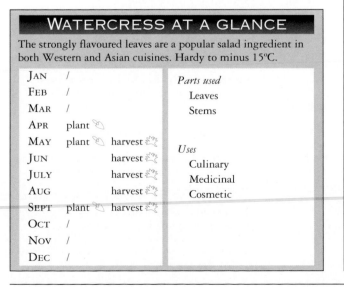

WATERCRESS AT A GLANCE

The strongly flavoured leaves are a popular salad ingredient in both Western and Asian cuisines. Hardy to minus 15°C.

JAN	/		
FEB	/		
MAR	/		
APR	plant 🌱		
MAY	plant 🌱	harvest 🌿	
JUN		harvest 🌿	
JULY		harvest 🌿	
AUG		harvest 🌿	
SEPT	plant 🌱	harvest 🌿	
OCT	/		
NOV	/		
DEC	/		

Parts used
Leaves
Stems

Uses
Culinary
Medicinal
Cosmetic

WORMWOOD
Artemisia

FEATURES

There are many species of artemisia, all with aromatic foliage and pleasant, but not particularly showy, yellow flowers. Wormwood, *A. absinthium*, is an extremely bitter plant with finely divided leaves. The related *A. abrotanum*, is also known as southernwood, or lad's love. There are many ornamental garden artemisias. Sizes and habits, however, vary enormously between species, some being ground-huggers, others being medium-sized, upright shrubs. Leaf shape and colour varies, too, and combinations of different artemisias can make very attractive plantings with a silver and grey theme.

CONDITIONS

Aspect Full sun is essential, as is an open position to ensure good air movement around the plant.

Site Grows best in moderately fertile, very well-drained soil that contains a small proportion of well-rotted organic matter.

GROWING METHOD

Sowing and planting Wormwood can be started from cuttings taken in late spring and rooted in small pots of moist, sandy potting mix kept in a bright but not fully sunny spot. It may also be grown from seed sown in spring just beneath the surface, either where plants are to grow or in pots or trays of seed compost.

Feeding Very little water is needed except in very dry summers. A mulch of well-rotted manure or compost laid under and beyond the plant's foliage canopy (but not right up against the trunk) is usually all the feeding required. Otherwise, sprinkle a handful of general fertiliser under the outer edge of the foliage canopy in early spring.

DESPITE ITS BITTERNESS, some artemisias were thought be be a potent aphrodisiac – hence the other name of 'lad's love'.

Problems Artemisias may sometimes suffer from blackfly. This can be treated with a liquid horticultural soap.

Pruning Cut herbaceous species of artemisia back to ground level in middle to late autumn or after frosts have started. Shrubby types may be sheared all over in early spring to make them more compact. Cut back hard in spring if the shrub has become too big and/or untidy.

HARVESTING

Picking Leaves are harvested by picking whole stems on a hot, dry morning in summer.

Storage Tie stems together and hang them upside down in a dim, airy place to dry. Dried leaves may be stored in airtight jars.

Freezing Not suitable for freezing.

USES

Culinary Although it is extremely bitter, wormwood was traditionally used to flavour wines and aperitifs such as absinthe and vermouth.

Medicinal *Caution:* different parts of different types of artemisia have various medicinal uses but do not take any of these herbs without the supervision of a trained herbalist.

Craft Wormwood has insect repellent properties and it can be used to make 'moth-repellent' sachets.

Gardening Wormwood, as all artemisias, has beautiful foliage and a pleasant aroma. A strong infusion of the leaves sprayed onto vegetables or ornamental plants repels caterpillars and snails; just having the plants nearby will drive some pests away.

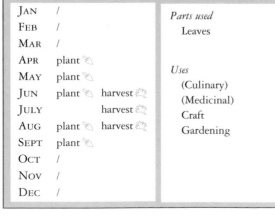

WORMWOOD AT A GLANCE

Perennial herb with decorative, finely divided silvery foliage, traditionally used to flavour absinthe. Hardy to minus 15°C.

JAN	/		
FEB	/		*Parts used*
MAR	/		Leaves
APR	plant		
MAY	plant		*Uses*
JUN	plant	harvest	(Culinary)
JULY		harvest	(Medicinal)
AUG	plant	harvest	Craft
SEPT	plant		Gardening
OCT	/		
NOV	/		
DEC	/		

YARROW
Achillea millefolium

FEATURES

Yarrow is a low, mat-forming perennial that has dense, dark green, fern-like foliage. Flat heads of small flowers appear on top of tall, mostly leafless stems during the later summer months and in autumn. They may be white, pink or yellow. This vigorous grower is well suited to growing in rockeries or on banks. Depending on the soil and situation in which it grows it can vary in height from 5cm (2in) to 60cm (24in).

CONDITIONS

Aspect Grow in full sun or light shade.
Site Well-drained, not-too-rich soil is ideal. Plants grow lax, flower poorly and die young in over-rich soil. They will rot if soil stays wet for long periods after rain or watering.

GROWING METHOD

Sowing and planting Establish yarrow in new areas by dividing the roots of mature plants in early spring or autumn. It may also be started from seed sown in spring in trays of moist seed compost. Just cover the seed and place the containers in a warm, bright but shaded spot until germination is complete. Gradually expose containers to more and more sun, and then transplant seedlings into their final site when they are big enough.

Feeding Water deeply but only occasionally. Yarrow does not require constant moisture as it has deep roots that will find water at lower levels in the soil. No feeding is necessary.

Problems No particular problems.
Pruning Cut plants to the ground in middle to late autumn or after frosts have started. New growth will appear in spring.

YARROW used to be grown in English churchyards to mock the dead, who supposedly were there because they hadn't eaten their yarrow broth.

HARVESTING

Picking Harvest leafy stems and flowers on a dry morning when plants are in the early stages of full bloom. Tie them together and hang them upside down in a dry, dim, airy place. If they are to be used to make dried arrangements, hang each flower stem separately.

Storage When the stems are dry, remove the flowers and leaves and break the leaves and stems into small pieces. Store these in airtight jars.

Freezing Not suitable for freezing.

USES

Culinary Young, small leaves have a slightly bitter flavour. Add a few chopped young leaves to salads or sandwiches for a piquant taste.

Medicinal Herbal tea made from the dried stems, leaves and flowers is a good general pick-me-up, blood cleanser, tonic for the kidneys, fever treatment and, reputedly, a slimming aid. Also used externally as wound healer.

Cosmetic An infusion can be used as a herbal skin cleanser.
Craft Flowers can be used in dried floral arrangements.
Gardening Although considered a weed in lawns, yarrow is an excellent companion plant, increasing the disease resistance of nearby plants and increasing their flavour and fragrance. It has been called the 'plant doctor'. Add it to the compost heap to speed rotting.

YARROW AT A GLANCE		
Although considered a weed by many, yarrow is an excellent companion plant and herbal tonic. Hardy to minus 15°C or below.		

JAN	/	
FEB	/	
MAR	plant	*Parts used*
APR	plant	Leaves
MAY	plant harvest	Stems
JUN	harvest	Flowers
JULY	harvest	
AUG	harvest	*Uses*
SEPT	plant	Culinary
OCT	/	Medicinal
NOV	/	Cosmetic
DEC	/	Craft
		Gardening

HERBS FOR THE KITCHEN

For thousands of years herbs have been indispensable additions to the cooking pot. Their incomparable fragrances and flavours can also be captured in herb butters, used to enliven vinegars and combined to make fines herbes *and* bouquet garni — *essentials in any well-stocked pantry. Herbs are also reputed to have soothing and healing properties when taken in herb teas.*

A thriving herb garden will allow you to experiment and create your own delicious recipes. Use them fresh or dried (see page 84 for instructions on how to dry herbs), but remember that fresh herbs are often less sharp in flavour then dried ones. Herbs can also vary in strength according to the season, so do taste as you add them to a recipe. And if the garden is overflowing with herbs, why not turn them into gifts for your friends and family: the butters, vinegars, teas and other recipes in this section will get you started.

LEFT: Herbs are not indoor plants but a sunny spot on the verandah just outside the kitchen is ideal — and very convenient. When grown in pretty painted pots like here they even become a decorative feature.

Herbal Teas

Herbal teas are growing in popularity. They can be made from one herb or a mixture of several, with flowers or spices added if desired. Some teas are made from herb flowers such as chamomile, others such as aniseed, dandelion and ginger are made from seeds, roots or bark. Tisanes are teas that have been brewed from the leaves of herbs.

Certain herbs have a stronger flavour than others and so less is needed, but in general about 3 teaspoons of chopped herbs is sufficient for one cup. If the herbs have been dried, they are already concentrated and no more than a level teaspooon is necessary. Herbal teas can be made by infusion, in much the same way as normal tea. Steep 2–3 teaspoons of leaves in very hot water for five minutes, being sure to keep the infusion covered to prevent the escape of steam. (If you use a teapot, keep it just for herbal teas.) Then use a strainer as you pour it

into the cup. Teas can also be made by decoction, which involves boiling herb seeds, roots or bark and some leaves in water for 15–20 minutes to draw out the flavours.

Herbal teas may be served hot or cold. If they are served iced, they should be made slightly stronger to allow for dilution as the ice cubes melt. For variety and a wonderful blend of flavours, fresh fruit juice can be added to cold teas. Sugar or honey can be added to teas as a sweetener, but most herbal teas are perfect as they are.

HERBAL TEAS can replace more conventional tea and coffee on any occasion. Drink them in the morning, for lunch or afternoon tea, or after dinner.

ANGELICA TEA

Infuse 3 teaspoons of fresh chopped leaves in 1 cup of boiling water for a calming drink, perfect before sleeping. This tea should not be taken by diabetics (because of its sugar content) or pregnant women, but it is a useful remedy for indigestion, coughs, colds, flatulence and rheumatism.

BASIL TEA

Infuse 3 teaspoons of fresh chopped leaves in 1 cup of boiling water. Basil tea is used to reduce travel sickness and morning sickness in pregnant women.

BERGAMOT TEA

Infuse 3 teaspoons of fresh leaves and flowers in 1 cup of boiling water. Use bergamot tea for sore throats and chest ailments.

CARAWAY TEA

Pour 1 cup of boiling water over 2 teaspoons of crushed seeds and let it steep for 5 minutes. Strain before drinking. Caraway tea is beneficial for the kidneys, glands and to aid digestion. It can also help to relieve flatulence.

CHAMOMILE TEA

Add dried or fresh chamomile flowers to a saucepan of boiling water, cover and simmer for 1 minute. Remove from the heat and let stand for a few minutes; then strain and drink. Do not drink large quantities of this tea, and it should be avoided in pregnancy. Chamomile tea is excellent as a relaxing bedtime drink, for relieving tension or menstrual pain.

DANDELION TEA

Infuse 5–6 leaves (remove stems and shred leaves first) in 1 cup of boiling water for a tasty drink that acts as a diuretic and mild laxative. This tea is often useful for relieving the symptoms of rheumatism.

DILL TEA

Pour 1 cup of boiling water over 2 teaspoons of crushed seeds and let it steep for 5 minutes. Strain before drinking. Dill seed tea has many uses, for poor digestion, flatulence, indigestion and stomach upsets, and as a mild tranquilliser and sleep inducer.

FENNEL TEA

Pour 1 cup of boiling water over 2 teaspoons of crushed seeds and let it steep for 5 minutes. Strain before drinking. This is a mild diuretic and laxative, and relieves indigestion, or pads of cotton wool can be soaked in cool tea and dabbed on eyelids to relieve tired eyes. Avoid consuming large amounts of fennel tea during pregnancy.

LEMON BALM TEA

Infuse 3 teaspoons of fresh leaves in 1 cup of boiling water. Lemon balm tea relieves indigestion, headaches and toothache, as well as tension, and it can help in the early stages of a cold.

LEMON GRASS TEA

Tie a piece of lemon grass into a knot and infuse it in 1 cup of boiling water. This mild diuretic also helps clear the skin.

LOVAGE TEA

Infuse 3 teaspoons of fresh leaves or 1 teaspoon of dried leaves in 1 cup of boiling water. A very mild diuretic, lovage tea is good for the kidneys and stimulates the appetite. Do not take large quantities during pregnancy.

MINT TEA

Infuse 3 teaspoons of fresh spearmint or peppermint leaves or 1 teaspoon of dried leaves in 1 cup of boiling water. Mint tea clears the head and sweetens the breath, and it is good for the digestion and colds. It can be drunk hot, or cold with ice cubes and lemon slices. Spearmint is milder than peppermint but more fragrant.

PARSLEY TEA

Infuse 3 teaspoons of fresh leaves or 1 teaspoon of dried leaves in 1 cup of boiling water. Drunk hot, parsley tea is a diuretic and it will help those suffering from anaemia. Avoid during pregnancy.

ROSEMARY TEA

Infuse 3 teaspoons of fresh leaves in 1 cup of boiling water. This tea is used for headaches, to improve the memory, as an aid to digestion and as a bedtime drink.

SAGE TEA

Infuse 3 teaspoons of fresh leaves in 1 cup of boiling water. Sage tea is used for sore throats, inflamed gums, constipation and rheumatism and is good for the liver and general health. Epileptics and pregnant women should avoid this tea.

SAVORY TEA

Infuse 3 teaspoons of fresh leaves or 1 teaspoon of dried leaves in 1 cup of boiling water. Either summer or winter savory can be used as a general tonic.

THYME TEA

Infuse 3 teaspoons of fresh leaves or 1 teaspoon of dried leaves in 1 cup of boiling water. Thyme tea is used for tension headaches, overtiredness, sore throats, colds or exposure to smokey atmospheres. It should be avoided during pregnancy. Cooled thyme tea can be used as a mouthwash.

CONDIMENTS

FRESH FROM THE GARDEN, herbs are a delightful addition to a variety of foods and condiments. Pick them as you need them.

HERB VINEGARS

Freshly picked herbs are a wonderful addition to a good white wine vinegar or cider vinegar. Herb vinegars add flavour and variety to salad dressings, marinades and sauces.

Pick the herbs, wash them and pat them dry. Loosely fill a clean jar with them, pour on enough vinegar to fill the jar and cap. Store in a warm place for about three weeks or until the vinegar is fully flavoured. If a stronger taste is required, strain and add fresh herbs. When the vinegar is ready, strain it and pour it into attractive bottles. Label the bottles, and add a fresh sprig of the herb to the bottle for decoration and identification.

Suitable herbs include basil, chives, dill, fennel, garlic, lovage, marjoram, mint, oregano, rosemary, sage, savory, tarragon or thyme.

HERB BUTTERS

Many herbs don't freeze particularly well, and one of the best ways of preserving their flavour for future use is to make a herb butter, which can be frozen for up to three months. The butters can then be used on breadsticks, pasta, vegetables, fish, grilled or barbecued meats.

Suitable herbs for making butters are basil, chervil, chives, dill, garlic, lovage, oregano, parsley, rosemary, sage, tarragon and thyme. Herbs can also be used in combination, for example basil, chives and oregano, or dill, chives and parsley.

For every 250g (8oz) of softened butter, mix in three tablespoons of freshly chopped herbs and the juice of one lemon. Pound the butter until smooth and roll into logs. Wrap in plastic film or foil, and freeze. Or the butter can be frozen in ice cube trays to make smaller portions.

FRESH BOUQUET GARNI

A bouquet garni is a small bunch of fresh herbs used to flavour stocks, soups, stews and sauces. To make one, tie together two sprigs of parsley, a sprig of thyme and a bay leaf. A sprig of marjoram, rosemary or sage and a piece of celery is sometimes included. Remove and discard the bouquet garni once the dish is cooked. If you prefer, chop the herbs and place them on a small square (about 15 cm square) of muslin. Gather the corners together and tie with a long string that can be left dangling over the edge of the pot for easy removal.

Bouquet garni can also be made from herbs that have been dried for a few days first.

FINES HERBES

This useful seasoning is a fine addition to any kitchen and a jar of *fines herbes* makes a good gift. Use them in small quantities in vegetable, egg, chicken and fish dishes, or in soups, salads and sauces. Add them at the end of cooking to retain their fresh flavour.

Finely chop equal quantities of chervil, chives, tarragon and, if desired, parsley.

CRYSTALLISED FLOWERS

Newly opened borage or violet flowers can be crystallised and used to decorate cakes and desserts. Take off the stems and handle the flowers as little as possible. Place them on greaseproof paper and brush the petals lightly with egg white. Use a small paintbrush and be sure to coat them well. Dust them with caster sugar and leave them to dry at room temperature. Store in an airtight container.

USING HERBS IN COOKING

ASIAN DISHES

fresh basil leaves;
fresh coriander leaves,
stems and roots;
garlic chives;
garlic;
fresh lemon grass;

BEANS

bay leaves; coriander
seeds; garlic; mint;
parsley; savory

BEEF

basil; bay leaves;
coriander leaves and
seeds; garlic; ginger;
horseradish; mint;
oregano; parsley;
thyme

BISCUITS

anise; dill or fennel seeds

BREAD

anise; dill or fennel seeds

CABBAGE

anise; dried basil;
dill and fennel seeds

CAKES

anise; dill or fennel
seeds; candied angelica
stems and crystallised
violet, dianthus or
borage flowers for
decorating

CHEESE

basil; fresh chervil;
chives; fresh dill;
garlic; oregano;
fresh parsley;
fresh rocket;
thyme

CHICKEN

basil; fresh chervil;
chives; fresh coriander
leaves, stems and roots;
coriander seeds;
garlic;
fresh lemon balm;
fresh lemon grass;
marjoram; oregano;
parsley; rosemary; sage;
savory; tarragon; thyme

EGGS

basil; fresh chervil;
chives; dill; marjoram;
oregano; parsley; savory;
tarragon; thyme

FISH

basil; chervil; chives;
coriander leaves and
seeds; dill; fennel leaves,
seeds and bulb; garlic;
horseradish;
fresh lemon balm;
fresh lemon grass;
marjoram; oregano;
parsley; fresh rocket;
tarragon; thyme

FRENCH DISHES

bay leaves; chervil;
chives; garlic; parsley;
rosemary; sage;
tarragon; thyme

FRUIT

fresh bergamot leaves
and flowers;
fresh young borage leaves
and flowers;
fresh lemon balm leaves;
fresh lemon verbena
leaves

GAME

bay leaves; fresh parsley;
rosemary

INDIAN DISHES

coriander seeds;
curry leaves;
fennel seeds; garlic;

ITALIAN DISHES

anise seed; basil;
chicory; fennel leaves,
seeds and bulb;
garlic; marjoram;
oregano; parsley;
fresh rocket;
rosemary; sage;
savory; thyme

LAMB

basil; bay leaves;
coriander leaves and
seeds; dill; garlic;
lemon balm;
marjoram; mint;
parsley; rosemary;
thyme

MEXICAN DISHES

coriander leaves and
seeds; oregano;
parsley

PICKLES

anise; coriander;
dill and fennel seeds;
ginger; garlic

PORK

anise leaves and seeds;
coriander leaves and
seeds; dill leaves and
seeds; garlic;
marjoram; oregano;
sage; thyme

POTATOES

chives; dill leaves; garlic;
parsley; rosemary; thyme

SALAD DRESSINGS

basil; chives; coriander;
dill; garlic; horseradish;
lemon grass; mint;
parsley; rosemary;
tarragon; thyme

SALADS

(all fresh) basil;
bergamot leaves and
flowers; young borage
leaves and flowers;
chervil; young chicory
leaves; coriander;
young dandelion leaves;
finely sliced fennel bulb;
nasturtium leaves and
flowers; parsley; rocket;
salad burnet; watercress

SAUCES

basil; bay leaves;
chives; dill; garlic; mint;
parsley; sage; tarragon

SHELLFISH

basil; chervil; chives;
coriander; dill;
lemon grass; parsley;
tarragon; thyme

TOMATOES

basil; chives; garlic;
marjoram; oregano;
parsley; rocket; thyme

VEAL

basil; garlic; marjoram;
oregano; parsley; sage;
rosemary; tarragon;
thyme

Note: Leaves used can be either fresh or dried unless specified; seeds can be used whole or ground unless specified.

HERB CRAFTS

Lavender, rosemary, thyme, oregano,
sage and marjoram are among
the most popular herbs for use in craft
and cosmetics. They can be used alone
to yield a fresh, clean aroma, or
combined with flowers such as roses
and scented-leaved geraniums for
a sweeter, gentler fragrance.

Used fresh or dried, herbs are remarkably versatile. In medieval England they were strewn on the floor to counteract unwelcome odours, and they can still be used to perfume the house. Make them into wonderful wreaths or wall hangings, potpourris or sachets. Herbs can be used to perfume the bath, to scent pillows or make skin fresheners, hair rinses or other cosmetics. In fact, they can be readily substituted for **flowers** in almost any craft idea.

LEFT: Herbs will add a delightful fragrance to many craft items:
there's plenty to choose from, ranging from scents that are cool and
refreshing to those that are sweet and pervasive.

ABOVE: A pot of sage.

DRYING HERBS

Fresh herbs are more attractive than dried ones and are almost always used in preference to the dried variety. However, you may want to cut and dry herbs that are annuals before they die down, or preserve the cut-away stems of shrubby herbs pruned at the end of summer. Some of the best herbs for drying are bay, thyme, rosemary, marjoram, oregano and sage.

Harvest the herbs on a dry day and divide them into small bunches. Strip a few leaves away from the base of the stem so that they can be tied in neat bunches without mould forming on the stems. Tie the stems firmly and hang the bunches in a warm, airy place away from direct sunlight. Leaves and flowers can also be dried spread on wire racks, paper or in shallow baskets. Place the containers in a dry, airy place away from light and gently toss the material each day to help the drying process. When they are completely dry, carefully strip the leaves from the branches and store them in labelled, airtight jars.

HERB POT-POURRIS

Wonderful, fragrant pot-pourris can be made from herbs, usually combined with rose petals or scented geranium leaves. They are perfect fillings for sachets or pillows, or can be placed in bowls or boxes to perfume the house.

Dry the herbs and flowers as described in the box opposite. Fixatives, such as oakmoss and dried orris root, and essential oils can be purchased from health food shops, some Asian supermarkets and some craft shops.

FLORAL AND HERB POT-POURRI

1 cup rose petals
¼ cup violets
½ cup marigold flowers
½ cup lavender
¼ cup cornflowers
½ cup sweet mixed herbs
1 tablespoon orris root powder
2 teaspoons cinnamon powder
5 drops rose oil
3 drops lavender oil
2 drops lemon oil

Place the dried flowers and herbs in a bowl and gently mix them together with a wooden spoon, being careful not to break the flower petals. Place the orris root and cinnamon in another bowl and, using an eyedropper, add the essential oils. Mix together thoroughly.

Add the orris root and cinnamon mixture to the dried materials and stir with a wooden spoon. Place in a brown paper bag, fold over the top and fasten with a clothes peg. Store in a cool, dark place for two to four weeks and shake the bag gently every few days to blend ingredients. It should then be ready for use.

LEMON SCENTED POT-POURRI

4 cups lemon verbena leaves
1 cup lemon-scented geranium leaves
½ cup basil
½ cup lemon thyme
½ cup dried lemon peel (freshly ground)
½ cup dried orange peel (freshly ground)
½ cup caraway seed
1 cup oakmoss
2 drops lemon verbena oil
2 drops bergamot oil

Mix the leaves together. Mix the peel with the caraway seed. Tear oakmoss into small pieces, place in a bowl and add essential oils. Rub the oil through the oakmoss and mix thoroughly with the leaves, peel and seeds. Place in an airtight container for about a month, stirring occasionally. It will then be ready for use.

LAVENDER AND HERB POT-POURRI

5 cups lavender flowers
1 cup lavender foliage
1 cup mint
1 cup rosemary
1 cup oakmoss
½ cup juniper berries, crushed
½ cup coriander seeds, crushed
2 drops lavender oil

Mix lavender flowers and leaves, and herbs in a bowl. In a separate bowl mix oakmoss, juniper berries and coriander, then add lavender oil and blend it through with your hands. Add this to the dried mixture and mix thoroughly. Store in an airtight container for about a month to allow the scents to mature, stirring occasionally. It will then be ready for use.

LAVENDER MIXTURE

2 cups lavender flowers
2 tablespoons orris root powder
4 drops lavender oil

Mix the flowers and orris root together and then add the oil and mix through. Store in an airtight container for three weeks, shaking occasionally, before using it.

ABOVE: This blue and white bowl is the perfect container for rose-based pot-pourri.

OPPOSITE PAGE: Pot-pourri ingredients, including bay leaves, rosemary, rose petals, lavender and orange peel.

FRAGRANT SACHETS

Small bags filled with pot-pourri mixtures make a fragrant addition to any home. Use them to perfume cupboards, drawers, storage areas or bags, or tie them on doorknobs or chair backs for a decorative effect.

MAKING A SACHET

A sachet is simply a fabric bag, made from a rectangle of fabric folded in half and stitched up two sides. The open side can then be hemmed or trimmed with lace, before the fragrant mixture is added and the bag tied off with a ribbon. Sachets can also be made from a handkerchief or other squares of fabric. Just put a spoonful of the mixture in the centre of the handkerchief, gather up the corners and tie them together with a pretty ribbon.

Moth sachet
A sachet filled with this mixture will repel moths for up to a year. Make several and tuck them among your woollen clothes and stored blankets.

1 cup rosemary
1 cup tansy
1 cup thyme
1 cup mint
1 cup southernwood
½ cup cloves (freshly ground)
½ cup dried lemon peel (freshly ground)

Crumble all the herbs together and mix with the cloves and lemon peel. Spoon the mixture into sachets and tie with a ribbon.

HERB PILLOW

Some herbs are thought to promote peaceful sleep and sweet dreams, and so a pillow filled with sleep-inducing herbs can be a practical addition to the home. Make this elegant little pillow to put inside a pillowcase or beside the bed, or the mixture can be put into a sachet that is tucked into the pillowcase with your usual pillow.

Make the pillow from two pieces of fabric 30x23cm (12x9in). Place the pieces together with right sides facing and stitch around three sides. If you want to add braid to the pillow, stitch it around the edges of one of the fabric pieces before sewing them together. Turn under the open edges about 1.2cm (0.5in) and stitch press studs along the turned under edges to close the pillow. Fill pillow with the herb mixture and close it.

If you want the pillow to be reusable, make a muslin insert for the fabric pillow. Make it in the same way as the pillow but slightly smaller all around. Put the mixture into the insert and stitch it closed; then slip it inside the pillow. The insert can then be discarded and replaced with a fresh one whenever necessary.

Herb mixture
1 cup dried rosemary
1 cup dried lavender
1 cup dried lemon verbena
1 cup dried lemon thyme
3 cups dried scented geranium leaves

Mix the materials together in a large bowl. If desired, a preservative such as orris root and a drop or two of essential oil can be added (follow the recipes for pot-pourri on page 85).

BATH BAGS

Bath bags are sachets made from muslin and tied with raffia or string. Tie one to the bath taps and let the water run over the bag – the water will be scented and you will feel relaxed and calm.

The bath bag is used only once, so make the bag small (about 10x5cm (4x2in) is a good size); make half a dozen or so at a time.

Oatmeal mixture
1 cup oatmeal
1 cup mixed herbs (rosemary, lemon verbena, sage or bay leaf)

Mix the ingredients together in a bowl. Spoon the mixture into the muslin bags and tie them closed. This oatmeal mixture will soften the skin.

Herb mixture
Bath bags can also be made using 2 tablespoons of bran and 1 tablespoon of a herb (lavender, chamomile or rosemary are good choices).

OPPOSITE PAGE. TOP: Sachets filled with herbal mixtures are a delightful way to scent underwear or linen. Make them from coarse-weave cottons, as here, or laces, brocades or muslins – anything that will allow the perfume through.

BOTTOM LEFT: Muslin bath bags can be filled with any herbal mixture to give a wonderfully indulgent bath.

BOTTOM RIGHT: This pillow is a beautiful addition to the bedroom, and when filled with sleep-inducing herbs it's useful, too.

HERB
WREATH
AND POSY

Herbs are well suited to wreaths and other arrangements, whether used fresh or dried, alone or mixed with flowers and foliage. Angelica, bay leaves, bergamot, fennel, lavender, lemon balm, rosemary, sorrel, thyme and wormwood are all useful. The arrangements shown here were made with fresh flowers to be used the same day, but similar ones can be made with dried herbs for a less colourful but longer lasting result.

HERB WREATH

This fresh herb wreath should be made on the day it is needed but it makes a lovely and unusual decoration for a dining area or for the front door. Herbs have been chosen to show a variety of colour — several different shades of green leaves and purple basil as well as the light blue flowers of rosemary, the purple ones of the basil and the bright orange of the nasturtiums — and texture, with curly parsley, soft dill and spikey thyme and rosemary.

Dill
Purple basil in flower
Rosemary in flower
Thyme
Parsley, curly and flat-leaved
Mint
Oregano
Nasturtium leaves and flowers
Foam base, 30cm (12in)in diameter
Green plastic
Stapler
Florists wire
Scissors

Cover the foam base with the green plastic and staple it in position — this will make it less obvious if any glimpses of the base are seen. Tie together small bunches (two or three sprigs) of each of the herbs, and wire each bunch together at the base of the stems, leaving 5cm (2in) lengths of wire at the ends. Push the wire ends into the foam base, starting at the top, slanting the bunches and working always in the same direction to give an impression of movement. Cover the top of the base and the top of the sides.

Space the different herbs around the circle to give a good mix of colours and textures. Tuck the last bunches under the first ones.

HERB POSY

This attractive and fragrant little posy would make a delightful table centre for a weekend lunch or outdoor meal, or it could be substituted for a posy of flowers. It is a worthy descendant of the old-fashioned tussie mussie, which was carried to ward off unpleasant smells. Although best when it is first made, this posy should last for several days.

Lavender in flower
Purple basil in flower
Thyme
Chives
Parsley, curly
Variegated rose geranium leaves

Rubber band or string
Length of raffia (optional)

Cut all the herbs with as long stems as is possible. Arrange the sprigs of lavender, basil, thyme and small bunches of the chives together, and then add the parsley and geranium leaves around the outside. Secure the stems with a rubber band and trim the stems to an even length. If desired, tie a length of raffia around the stems as a finishing touch.

ABOVE: This delightful herb posy makes an ideal table decoration for kitchen or dining room.

LEFT: Add colour and fragrance with this fresh herb wreath. It can be hung on a door to provide a special welcome, or on a wall to give an instant lift to any room.

Herbal Cosmetics

There are many simple herbal preparations that you can use to tone, clean, moisturise or simply refresh your skin. Hair rinses, too, can be quickly made from herbs.

CHAMOMILE FACE MASK

A very simple face mask can be made from chamomile flowers, honey and bran. It softens the skin and leaves it feeling beautifully smooth and refreshed.

Make an infusion (see page 78), using 1 tablespoon of dried chamomile flowers or 3 tablespoons of fresh ones and 1 cup of boiling water. Allow the infusion to stand for about half an hour and then strain.

Warm 1 teaspoon of honey in a pan and mix it with about 1/3 cup of the chamomile water and 2 tablespoons of bran. Spread it on your face, leave it for about 10 minutes and then wash it off.

FENNEL FACE CLEANSER

This fresh mixture made from fennel seed, buttermilk and honey is a lovely way to cleanse your face naturally.

Crush or roughly chop 1 tablespoon of fennel seed and then pour 1 cup of boiling water over it. Let it stand for about half an hour and then strain it into a small bowl.

Add 2 tablespoons of buttermilk and 1 teaspoon of honey to the fennel seed water and mix it all together.

Pour the resulting mixture into a completely clean container and refrigerate it until it is cool. The cleanser can be taken from the fridge as needed.

FEVERFEW MOISTURISER

This complexion milk serves as a moisturiser and will help to discourage blackheads and fade skin blemishes.

Place half a cup of fresh feverfew leaves and 1 cup of milk in a saucepan. Simmer for about 20 minutes and leave it to stand. Strain the liquid into a clean container and refrigerate.

Apply it to the skin with cotton balls and let it dry. Rinse off with lukewarm water.

TANSY-LEAF SKIN FRESHENER

This easy-to-make skin freshener has a strong tansy fragrance. Splash it onto your skin straight from the fridge.

Place 1 cup of fresh tansy leaves, 1 cup of water and 1 cup of milk in a small saucepan and bring to the boil. Simmer it for 15 minutes and then leave it to cool. Strain the liquid from the saucepan into a clean container and then refrigerate it.

HAIR RINSES

There are a number of herbs that make useful and fragrant hair rinses, to use after shampooing. Chamomile rinses will brighten fair hair, rosemary rinses will help control greasy hair and add shine to any hair, and sage rinses will darken grey hair.

Make the hair rinse by placing 5 cups of water and 1 cup of chamomile flowers, fresh rosemary tips or sage leaves in a saucepan and bring the mixture to the boil. Simmer it for 15 minutes and let it cool. The sage rinse should stand for several hours. Then strain and bottle it, ready for use.

Always use an old towel to dry your hair after using a herb rinse — sage, in particular, will stain the towel.

HERBAL COSMETICS are simple to make and much cheaper than purchased ones. Packaged in attractive bottles and provided with corks and colourful ribbons, they also make very desirable gifts.

PLANT NAME	SPRING			SUMMER			AUTUMN			WINTER		
	EARLY	MID	LATE	EARLY	MID	LATE	EARLY	MID	LATE	EARLY	MID	LATE
Alchemilla			●	●	●	●	●					
Aloe vera	●	●	●	●	●	●	●	●	●	●	●	●
Angelica			●	●	●	●	●	●				
Anise			●	●	●	●	●	●				
Anise hyssop			●	●	●	●						
Basil			●	●	●	●						
Bay tree	●	●	●	●	●	●	●	●	●	●	●	●
Bergamot			●	●	●	●	●					
Betony				●	●	●						
Borage			●	●	●	●	●					
Caraway			●	●	●	●						
Catmint			●	●	●	●	●					
Chamomile			●	●	●	●						
Chervil			●	●	●	●	●					
Chicory			●	●	●	●	●	●	●	●	●	●
Chives		●	●	●	●	●	●	●				
Comfrey			●	●	●	●	●	●				
Coriander			●	●	●	●	●	●				
Curry plant	●	●	●	●	●	●	●	●	●	●	●	●
Dandelion		●	●	●	●	●	●	●				
Dill			●	●	●	●	●	●				
Elder			●	●			●	●				
Fennel			●	●	●	●	●	●				
Feverfew			●	●	●	●	●					
Garlic				●	●	●	●	●				
Herb Robert			●	●	●	●	●					
Horehound			●	●	●	●	●					
Horseradish						●	●	●	●			
Hyssop			●	●	●	●	●					
Lavender			●	●	●	●						

PLANT NAME	SPRING			SUMMER			AUTUMN			WINTER		
	EARLY	MID	LATE	EARLY	MID	LATE	EARLY	MID	LATE	EARLY	MID	LATE
Lemon balm			🌿	🌿	🌿	🌿	🌿					
Lemon grass				🌿	🌿	🌿						
Lemon verbena			🌿	🌿	🌿	🌿	🌿					
Lovage			🌿	🌿	🌿	🌿	🌿	🌿				
Marjoram			🌿	🌿	🌿	🌿	🌿					
Mint			🌿	🌿	🌿	🌿	🌿					
Nasturtium			🌿	🌿	🌿	🌿	🌿	🌿				
Oenothera			🌿	🌿	🌿	🌿	🌿	🌿				
Oregano			🌿	🌿	🌿	🌿	🌿	🌿				
Parsley		🌿	🌿	🌿	🌿	🌿	🌿	🌿	🌿			
Pinks			🌿	🌿	🌿							
Pot marigold			🌿	🌿	🌿	🌿						
Purslane				🌿	🌿	🌿	🌿					
Rosa gallica				🌿	🌿		🌿	🌿				
Rosemary	🌿	🌿	🌿	🌿	🌿	🌿	🌿	🌿	🌿	🌿	🌿	🌿
Rue	🌿	🌿	🌿	🌿	🌿	🌿	🌿	🌿	🌿	🌿	🌿	🌿
Sage	🌿	🌿	🌿	🌿	🌿	🌿	🌿	🌿	🌿			
Salad burnet			🌿	🌿	🌿	🌿						
Salad rocket		🌿	🌿	🌿	🌿	🌿	🌿	🌿				
Santolina	🌿	🌿	🌿	🌿	🌿	🌿	🌿	🌿	🌿	🌿	🌿	🌿
Savory	🌿	🌿	🌿	🌿	🌿	🌿	🌿	🌿	🌿	🌿	🌿	🌿
Sorrel		🌿	🌿	🌿	🌿	🌿	🌿	🌿				
Tansy		🌿	🌿	🌿	🌿	🌿	🌿	🌿				
Tarragon			🌿	🌿	🌿	🌿	🌿					
Thyme	🌿	🌿	🌿	🌿	🌿	🌿	🌿	🌿	🌿	🌿	🌿	🌿
Valerian							🌿	🌿				
Violet	🌿	🌿	🌿	🌿	🌿	🌿						🌿
Watercress			🌿	🌿	🌿	🌿	🌿					
Wormwood				🌿	🌿	🌿						
Yarrow			🌿	🌿	🌿	🌿						

INDEX

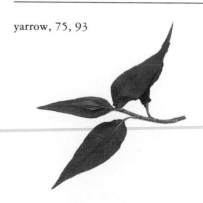

Published by Murdoch Books UK Ltd, 1998
Ferry House, 51-57 Lacy Road, Putney, London SW15 1PR

This edition published 2001 for INDEX: Henson Way,
Kettering, NN16 8PX, United Kingdom

ISBN 1-897730-81-0

Printed by Toppan in China.

SERIES EDITOR: Graham Strong

EDITOR: Valerie Duncan

TEXT: Geoffrey Burnie and John Fenton-Smith

DESIGNER: Karen Awadzi

CREATIVE DIRECTOR: Marylouise Brammer

MANAGING EDITOR: Christine Eslick

COMMISSIONING EDITOR: Helen Griffin

PUBLISHER: Anne Wilson

PHOTOGRAPHS: All photographs by Lorna Rose except Geoffrey Burnie (pp17, 19);
Denise Grieg (pp24L, 24R, 47); Stirling Macoboy (pp36, 38, 60 lower R);
Andre Martin (pp76-77, 79-91); Luis Martin (p78); Reg Morrison (p11);
Clive Nichols Garden Pictures (front cover); Mr. Fothergill's (p27);
Graham Strong (pp12, 15); Pat Brindley (pp30, 58); Michael Warren (p71).
Identification pictures by Graham Strong, Reg Morrison, Luis Martin,
Geoffrey Burnie and Lorna Rose.

COVER: The edible flowers and leaves of chives
TITLE PAGE: lavender